UNLEASH THE GLORY

By PASTOR ONSLOW ROSS

The events and conversations in this book have been set down to the best of the author's ability, although some names and details have been changed to protect the privacy of individuals.

ISBN: 978-1-09834-661-4

Foreword

In Macon, Georgia, the founder, and brethren of a church was being bullied by the local bank. Eventually, he would discover that this institution had become rich...well richer, through illegal activity.

To this day, he still does not understand how a FDIC approved institution, was able to circumvent not only federal banking laws but real estate practices as well. Then they targeted him for criminal prosecution, in a federal insurance fraud case.

As he unfolds his story, he also faces his own demons, as he discusses the struggles and hardships which he faced both before and during his incarceration. He acknowledges that although he grew up in a Christian environment with ministry leaders that spanned generations, that did not exclude him from the trials of human nature.

"As I overcame drug addiction," states I Am Sir O, "It took me time to be able to travel the path that God called me to accomplish."

As mass incarceration continues in our country, even of non-violent offenders, and as harsher lengthy prison sentences become more common, here is his story.

- Chris.

Introduction

God has given me the gift of an excellent memory, which allows me the ability to tell this story. It is a story that is over three decades in the making. I thank God for giving me the gift, and the ability to share, hoping it will shed some light, and be a blessing to some.

The story I am about to share with you is one of how I was tested in so many ways throughout my life. You would say that life tried to break me and take me out, but it was through God's strength I made it through.

God had brought me out of the depths of drug addiction to the pulpit, where I've ministered to thousands, and basked in the glow of knowing I was making a difference in the lives of others. You can say that I had a valley to the mountaintop experience.

Now, from the pulpit to an inmate in a federal correctional facility. A place where I was no longer recognized for my relationship with God but seen as a number in the many that society has counted out. I question "why this was happening to me?" and surely knew that it was all a misunderstanding that would sort itself out.

After a trial which I believed would exonerate not only my name, but my reputation, and calling, I stood convicted of crimes I did not commit. Not understanding how this could happen to me, I struggled. I struggled with understanding the plan that God had in store for my life. Although I know that God's wisdom is greater than our own, I was still looking for answers.

That is why I have to share with you my story. The story of a man whose name was dragged through the mud and left standing all alone to talk the fall for someone's error. It's unfolding before your eyes. From this story, you learn that even amid turmoil and strife, God's light always shines through. There is hope for us all.

"Walk your divine destiny" is my story. It's my journey of how, despite my sordid past, God trusted me to be in charge of many, then in a blink of an eye I was battling hell. A battle that tried to break me but matured me and taught me what all I was capable of.

Ten years in federal prison is just that, *hell*! Words could never describe the impact prison had on my life. Mentally, it has been an experience I would not wish on my worst enemy. I have lost so much. However, God has shown me how only He can take tragedy and turn it into triumph; it's where His glory shines through.

Please use my story and apply the lessons learned to your life. For some, experience is the best teacher, but for those who are wise, they can learn from other people's mistakes. You are wise, so learn from my mistakes so you can give live more consciously each day, stay committed to your growth and live in alignment with your purpose.

-I Am Sir O

Table of Contents

Chapter 1

Chasing Destiny

Joseph had a dream, and when he told it to his brothers,
they hated him all the more. This is the account of
Jacob's family line. Joseph, a young man of seventeen,
was tending the flocks with his brothers, the sons of
Bilhah and the sons of Zilpah, his father's wives, and he
brought their father a bad report about them.

Genesis 37:2,5 (NIV)

It is clear, Joseph's story is not his alone, but that of his
lineage. Joseph was a child of the forefathers of our
faith, Abraham, Isaac, and Israel. He dreamt of
greatness, a greatness he was destined for. Like Joseph's
parentage, many came before me and paved the way that
would lead me to my destiny. I, too, dreamt of greatness.

"What we call our destiny is truly our character and that
character can be altered. The knowledge that we are
responsible for our actions and attitudes does not need to
be discouraging, because it also means that we are free
to change this destiny. One is not in bondage to the past,

which has shaped our feelings, to race, inheritance, background. All this can be altered if we have the courage to examine how it formed us. We can alter the chemistry provided we have the courage to dissect the elements."

-Anais Nin, The Diary of Anaïs Nin, Vol. 1: 1931-1934

Ever since I was a child, I wanted to follow the footsteps of my grandfather and father. I would hear them speak and see the transformation of the hearts and minds of the congregation, Sunday after Sunday. I admired their hard work and tenacity to preach the unadulterated word of God. Yes, these were the men I wanted to emulate.

My father began his ministry when I was 13 years old. I recall vividly my father sitting down with me and encouraging me to continue the family legacy he and my grandfather had built. He wanted me to preach, following the path of my forefathers. However, like my mother, he wanted the best for me no matter what I pursued. Luckily, as I went through my life, I was surrounded by people whose faith was an inspiration to myself and others. My grandparents; parents; aunts; and uncles were all conservative and traditional Christians who enjoyed serving God and other people.

My parents were married for over 42 years. They both made significant sacrifices for the ministry and their family. My Mother Evelyn is the most pleasant, beloved, generous, hardworking, independent woman I know. She worked in the medical field for over 30 years. Caring for people naturally came to her.

My mother did all the things she needed to do to get the things she wanted or to provide for her family. She was a woman full of wisdom. You could not just approach with words; you would have to put action behind everything you presented to her. She encouraged me to chase my dreams and would support me in any career path I chose, but she knew that ministry was embedded in me.

Willie was my magnificent father. He was a 'stand-up guy' who was loved and respected by many. I admired and looked up to my father, for he was a wise man. My father was a master mason, with over 20 years of experience, that was disciplined, structured, and very outgoing. I am honored to have inherited some of his character traits.

I was raised in the Bloomfield community, in a two-bedroom home, that had a kitchen, a living room, and one bathroom. A house that took nine years for my parents to attain. In our neighborhood, people looked after each other and their children. The community embodied the saying, 'it takes a village to raise a child.' It was a community dear to me because most of my family members lived in this community.

To describe my young self as spoiled would be an understatement. My parents treated me like a prince throughout my home and at the ministry. I even had the pleasure of having my own royal chair in the pulpit and at the dining room table. However, as a privileged child of ministry leaders, much was expected of me. I could not do the same things other children were doing. I had to be an example for other kids my age. Growing up as a "church kid" had its challenges. Much was required of me.

My peers treated me differently as if I had the plague. I would get teased because of who my father was and how he raised me. We revered God in my house and manners were of the utmost importance, so my parents instilled certain things in me that weren't in other kids. I would get made fun of for saying grace over my lunch, saying "yes sir" and "yes ma'am," and opening doors for females was a given. It was like I was a target and some of the same kids that made fun of me in school, I would have to see them at church on Sunday.

At school, teachers would explain to me that I was ahead of my time. But, I knew that because I was raised a certain way, it was difficult for me to fit in. I was an average student, making average grades, but I wanted to be an ordinary kid, not a preacher's kid. I tried to fit in, to socialize, to hang out with the other kids and not have to worry about being an example for others to model. Over time, little by little, I explored different things trying to fit in. Trying those different things landed me into trouble. I was compromising what I believed in as a person and forgetting the values I had been taught.

Mrs. Rosa Mae, better known as "Granny," had the biggest heart for her family and all of humanity. Granny was a loyal mother, grandmother, and a wife who was married to Pop for over 60 years. I had a special place in her heart, and she would do anything in the world for me. Granny only lived a mile away, so I would often walk to her house.

Now, Granny was a woman above reproach. She did not party; she did not curse, and she never did drugs. When I was at the lowest point of my young adult years, Granny supported me and encouraged me. She would remind me, "Son, you are going through a phase; you will make it through this. God has a plan for your life."

There was never a moment when she wasn't there for me. She fed me and fed me well. Granny was a master chef who loved cooking for people. Everyone in the family would come to her for a recipe and instructions on cooking. I remember the delicious meals she prepared for me. She would make my favorite breakfast; eggs, toast, and the best pancakes in the world. When it came to dinner, my favorite meal was fried chicken, corn casserole, sweet potatoes, with banana pudding for dessert. Every year on my birthday, from childhood to adulthood, Granny made me a scrumptious strawberry cake. Cooking was a way she showed her love to her family. Family was everything to her.

Momma Doris, my mother's mother, is an incredible, loving, and caring woman. Momma Doris was very involved in my life. When I was on a downward spiral, in the wake of destruction, sitting in jail, she was the only person who came to see me. She would always send me money every month faithfully, which I was very grateful for. Every year, on every holiday, she would send me a card. Momma Doris is old-fashioned. She would rather receive a letter than accept a phone call any day.

I remember driving her to church every Sunday. We would never return home without visiting her late husband's tombstone, Felix. Grandpa Felix died when I was young, and although I did not get to know him personally, Momma Doris kept his name and spirit alive by telling stories about Felix, about how he was a good man from Louisiana.

These people instilled in me great values, wisdom, character, and integrity that would—little did I know—help shape my destiny.

Life Applications

We define destiny as the events that will happen to a particular person or thing in the future. It's crucial that you have the right people around you because of the words they speak over you, their actions, and the things they instill in you will help shape your destiny.

As a child, you don't always take heed to the instructions and wisdom of adults. You may feel as if they are "old" or "don't understand you" but know that life happens to us all and any words of wisdom given to you, hold on to them. They might just come in handy when you least expect it.

Being socially accepted is one of the greatest perceived needs for youth and young adults. You want to be liked. You want to fit in. Friends are important and are very influential in the teen years than at any other time in your life. Parents aren't around as much as peers are so in your youth you crave that validation and acceptance from your peers.

It's essential you know that real friends or things of substance will not ask or require you to compromise your beliefs. As adults, we can fall victim to compromising, too. To get a promotion, we change some numbers around on the report to make our quotas look better. Not to feel like we're further behind in life than our high school classmates, we tell a small lie to make ourselves look good. To get more back from Uncle Sam, we claim children that aren't ours. Compromising our values and beliefs isn't a youth thing, it's an integrity and self-worth issue that adults face too.

Have you ever heard of the saying, *"you don't have to lie to kick it?"* It means that you don't have to pretend to be someone else when you're around me. Be yourself. This is perhaps easier said than done for some people. Society shuns and isolates things they don't understand, but it takes a brave individual to go against the grain and create a trail where there once was none. Consider these great leaders in their perspective fields such as Dr. King, Muhammed Ali, and Oprah Winfrey.

People opposed them but they stood true to their beliefs and knew their worth. It can be hard and lonely standing up for your beliefs when others shame and isolate you. Therefore, it's important to have people to support, love, and encourage you along the way. My family was a big support system for me. Even if your family doesn't support you, you have friends or even organizations of like-minded individuals that can encourage you through your darkest hour. No matter who does or doesn't support you, it's important that you don't compromise on your beliefs. These beliefs are the building blocks that help shape your destiny.

Did you know?

A recent survey by the American Psychological Association says that 34% of teenage girls and 22% of teenage boys feel pressure to "be a certain way."[1] That's roughly 1 out of 3 girls and 1 out of 4 boys! Often as adults, we forget how it felt, but the pressure a youth can feel from their peers can be overwhelming at times. It's especially concerning today, as social media has risen to a place of almost absolute authority in young people's lives. That same survey by the APA discovered that 29% of teen boys reported feeling stressed about how others viewed them on social media, while an alarming 39% of girls described the same sentiment.[2] That's just a little bit shy of being 1 out of every 2 girls!

It can't be overstated then, just how important it is for youth to have a positive and healthy support system in their lives, outside of the friends they make at school or online. At home, we need to make every effort to encourage and talk to our children. They shouldn't have to go to their friends or coaches to find out who they are and how much they are valued. They shouldn't have to go on Facebook or Instagram to get their first encouragement for the day.

While these sources are not bad in and of themselves, it's more important our children know from the moment they wake up in their bed to the moment they lay down at night that they are loved, valued and cherished by their household. When this happens, much of the peer pressure that children feel can be countered more easily. They will have a strong, grounded assurance of who they are, and they will know they don't have to do or be anything that doesn't line up with who they have learned they are at home.

1. "Stress in America Press Room", n.d., accessed August 9, 2019, https://www.apa.org/news/press/releases/stress/.

2. "Stress in America Press Room", n.d., accessed August 9, 2019, https://www.apa.org/news/press/releases/stress/.

Chapter 2

The Fall

"... they took him and threw him into a pit.
The pit was empty; there was not water in it."

Genesis 37:24 (NKJV)

In his young adulthood, Joseph found himself at the
bottom of a pit, thirsty, with no way out. Only a
short time before, he had dreamed of greatness.
How was he to achieve the great
things he was destined for in this seemingly
hopeless place? In my teenage years, I found myself
in a pit that I had fallen into. A pit of
self-destruction, into which I had fallen and hit rock
bottom.

"Man learns through experience, and the spiritual
path is full of different kinds of experiences. He will
encounter many difficulties and obstacles, and they
are the very experiences he needs to encourage and
complete the cleansing process."

-Sai Baba

For the next three years, I managed to survive in middle school. I was miserable even though I maintained decent grades. When I graduated middle school, I saw high school as a fresh start, but some of the same people from middle school carried over their childish behavior as well as my "preacher's kid" nickname.

My mother noticed subtle changes in my behavior long before my father. I guess you would say that he was busy being a servant while my mother was busy looking after me. Ever since I got into high school, I was determined to create a path of my own. I no longer wanted to be known as the "preacher kid." I tried my best to run away from that name. I started hanging out in places that I knew weren't "good enough" for a child of a preacher. At first, they tried to kick me out and make fun of me, but one day, I got pushed too far.

After school, a guy tried me. He talked about my father, which I was used to, but he made a comment about my mother, and I warned him. I told him to stop, but he kept going. He made one to many jokes about my mother, and I gave him a good helping hand that knocked him out. I didn't even know I had that in me. I guess that punch was a result of all the years of bullying and he just picked the wrong day. After that day, they started taking me seriously. I wasn't known as the 'preacher's kid.' My parents never found out about the incident.

At 16 years old, my father brought me a brand new grey and white Nissan Polstar, just in time for the summer. I was beyond excited, though my mother was not too pleased. My mother instilled one rule and that was I had to be home before midnight.

I started out fine, but the longer I enjoyed my liberties, I started coming home at midnight, barely making curfew. I would enter through the back entryway, hoping not to wake anyone, but my mother would be in the living room sitting in her rocking chair. I would take a few steps on the stairs, and then she would turn on the living room light. She would call my name and ask me where I've been. I would give her the same response, "out with friends, but I made it home on time."

I only had the car for a few months before it drove me further to my self-destruction. One day, my father told me that my cousin was in town and that I should go visit him. I called him up, and we made plans to meet. It felt good to say that I was driving and I would pick him up. I picked him up at my aunt's house, and we headed out that night. He told his mom that we were heading to the movies, but we never made it.

On the way to the theatre, my cousin asked me if I had become a man yet. By the look on my face, he could tell that I was clueless as to what he meant. He laughed, and he said to me that he was going to "put me on." He pulled something out of his pocket that looked like a cigarette, but it was brown. He put it to his mouth and lit it. He took a deep inhale, held it in, and then blew it out to make it look like smokestacks. Then he passed it to me.

If my cousin was doing it and it was going to make me a man, then *why not*? I took one hit of it, and it felt like my lungs were on fire. I started choking, and my cousin burst out in laughter. "Aiight, aiight, aiight man, you're wasting it. You gone learn to puff and pass. You hear me? Puff, then pass." He said as he took the cigarette looking stick out of my hand.

I later learned that it was marijuana. I was too high to remember all of what we did that night. My cousin had to remind me the next day of all the stupid stuff I said and did. He told me not to get hooked because weed was an expensive habit, but yet the next night, we were back in my car, smoking weed. I found something I liked, and I love how it made me feel. When I was smoking weed, life seemed troubled free. Everything was good.

One night after we smoked, my cousin asked if I could hold a bag of his weed. He couldn't take it in the house because he knew someone would find it and smoke it. I agreed because that meant that it was guaranteed weed for me. Unbeknownst to me, my father decides to clean out my car and finds the bag of weed.

I never forget the look of disappointment on my father's face. It was like he couldn't ever imagine me doing drugs. I didn't apologize nor did I snitch on who the weed belonged to. I told my father that he shouldn't have been in my car in the first place. He looked at me but didn't recognize who I was. It was at that moment he realized that he had lost his son.

My parents decided that day to take the car away from me. That angered me, and I stormed out of the house. *How dare they take my car from me? I'm grown, I don't need them.* I thought. That day the spirit of rebellion had set in my heart.

Although I was blessed as a teenager, I took it for granted. Blinded by greed, I wanted more. I did not want to depend on others. I was selfish, mischievous, hard-headed, and stubborn. I disregarded the sacrifices that my family had made for me and ignored all they had taught me. I began to spiral out of control, and only God knew where I was headed.

I left home that night and didn't return until late in the evening the following day, and my father scolded me. He reminded me that he is the one that pays the bills and put a roof over my head. As my father yelled, I could hear my mother in the background, praying. Yet, each time I heard her call on the name of Jesus, it angered me. Where was Jesus when I was getting bullied? Where was Jesus when I needed him?

I sat there, hearing what my father was saying, but I wasn't listening. I was making a plan to leave this place as soon as I could. I was tired of being told what to do. Once he got done, I nodded and went to my room. The next morning, I dropped out of high school and enrolled at Ernest Solange Academy to take the GED test.

That summer, I did everything I could to fit in with my cousin and his friends. Even though they continued to treat me as an outsider in their group, I was just happy to have been around some older guys.

Because I was better off financially than others in the group, they used me to support their drug addiction. As long as I bought their weed, I could hang out with them. One night, one of the guys talked about trying something new. He heard about it from one of his homeboys and understood that it was good. They called up the dealer, and when the dealer came, I paid for it. One guy went to the back to fix it up. I was used to it. They would get the weed, one of them would go to the back, roll it up and get it ready. I would be the last to smoke as always.

I watched the guys take one hit after another and watched how their eyes lit up. I kept thinking it must be good the way they were responding. I took my first hit, and I see why the other guys' eyes lit up. That night, I went from smoking marijuana; to smoking cocaine inside a cigarette. That was the best high I had ever experienced, and it got me started on a chase. I tried to get the same high, but it never happened.

By the age of 19, I was a crack cocaine addict, smoking out of a can. My addiction resulted in several juvenile convictions. My first time going to the county jail, my father came and bailed me out. My parents thought my experience with the judicial system would straighten me out, but I was too much of an addict to stop. I kept chasing a high and doing whatever I could to get my next high. I kept going in and out of jail, and when I had a clear conscience, I would go right back to my parent's house. Strangely, the very same place I was trying to get away from.

One day when I was released from the county jail, I made my way back home, but this time was different. This time they had changed the locks. I knew my parents were there because I saw their car. I banged on the door, but no one responded. I pounded so much that I nearly got the door ajar. My behavior scared my mom because it was her voice that I heard yelped.

"Stop it, stop it right now. I don't know what has happened to you, but you aren't the man that we've raised. I've prayed and prayed for you, but you continue to be used by the enemy. You can fight this! I know you can, but you have to want to." She said as she got closer to the door. I stood there, listening. I heard her pain. Her frustration.

"Now, I love you, but I can't continue watching you do this. I've told your father to change the locks, so don't be mad at him. You have to fight this and get cleaned. Until then, you aren't welcomed here." I heard her heart break into pieces each tear she cried at the door. The weight of her words felt heavy on me, and I sat at the door and cried. The thought of me hurting my mother sobered me up, until I found the next dealer on the corner.

If my mother didn't want me, I might as well do what made me feel good. Made no sense for both of us to be hurt. I was left to fend for myself. I didn't have many people to turn to. I had cut my ties with the ministry, so that left me with very little options. I moved from one family member's house to the next. I went wherever a door would open until I overstayed my welcome.

Each time I got kicked out, I made sure to get my next high. I spent more and more time at the county jail, accumulating multiple misdemeanor charges. My future was bleak. The light that was in me was dwindling.

Life Applications

Throughout life, you will have many desires. The desire
to be rich, desire to lose weight, desire to own homes,
and much more. But be mindful that those desires, no
matter how good they are, don't lead you astray. Don't
get consumed by your desire that you lose sight of what
you already have. 1st John 2:16 (NIV) states "For
everything in the world—the lust of the flesh, the lust of
the eyes, and the pride of life—comes not from the
Father but from the world."

It is human nature to want more, to want bigger
and better, but at what cost. The cost of pursuing these
desires could cost you your life if you are not careful. I
advise you to take an evaluation of what you have. Have
a gratitude check. List everything in your life that you
have; work, family, car, housing, and write why you are
grateful for those things. If there is nothing you can find
that you are thankful for then, you need to do a
self-check.

Also, seeing a loved one inflicting pain upon
themselves, especially when you've done all that you
can do. It comes a time when you have to give them and
the situation over to God. Pray that they change and their
life becomes better, but it has to start with them wanting

it for themselves. You can't help someone that doesn't want help. You can only help them when they are ready.

If you find yourself in a situation in which you want a loved one to be free from addiction and you've done all that you know you could do, pray; and use these scriptures as reference.

- Let us hold unswervingly to the hope we profess, for he who promised is faithful. (Hebrews 10:23 NIV)
- We wait in hope for the Lord; he is our help and our shield. (Psalm 33:20 NIV)
- Fear not, for I am with you; be not dismayed, for I am your God. (Isaiah 41:10 NKJV)
- I will strengthen you, yes, I will help you, I will uphold you with My righteous right hand. (Isaiah 41:10 NKJV)
- "Come now, let us reason together," says the Lord. "Though your sins are like scarlet, they shall be as white as snow; though they are red as crimson, they shall be like wool."(Isaiah 1:18 NIV)

Don't give up and think that your prayers are in vain. They are not. Sometimes the situations that people put themselves in produce strongholds, and it will take the fervent prayers of the righteous to bring them out.

Did you know?

With school and extracurricular activities outside of the home playing such a pivotal role in today's society, it's important now more than ever for parents and families to make sure they are aware of their children's well-being. According to a research study in 2017, a reported 19% of youth in high school experienced bullying on school grounds, and 15% reported they were bullied online through electronic devices.[3] It's important to note these statistics only cover high school youth. We have to also consider that many children in middle and even elementary school have electronic devices now, and are therefore susceptible to all types of bullying as well.

Our children today are in contact with so many people at almost all times. With the rise of technology, it's become easier to miss signs of bullying, peer pressure, and even drug use. Emotional wounds can be hard to detect, especially when they're inflicted from behind a phone or computer late at night or early in the morning. And drug use seems to be able to easily escape the notice of parents and guardians until it becomes problematic. In 2013, a national survey reported that about 43% of adolescents from age 12 to 17 who used alcohol received substance abuse treatment for it, and about 66% received treatment for marijuana abuse.[4] That means for almost 1 out of every 2 young people who used alcohol and 2 out of 3 who used marijuana, they had to receive treatment for abusing the substance!

This points to an almost silent widespread problem that is attacking our youth, and for this reason we must make sure we are in constant communication with them. It might make them or even us feel uncomfortable for a moment, but it's imperative that we do it anyway. The temporary awkwardness will fade, and over time staying involved and in-the-know about our children's actions, feelings and thoughts could very well save their life.

3. "United States Adolescent Healthy Relationships Facts", HHS.Gov, August 2019, https://www.hhs.gov/ash/oah/facts-and-stats/national-and-state-data-sheets/healthy-adolescent-relationship-fact-sheets/united-states/index.html.

4. "America's Addiction to Opioids: Heroin and Prescription Drug Abuse ...", n.d., accessed August 11, 2019, https://www.drugabuse.gov/about-nida/legislative-activities/testimony-to-congress/2014/americas-addiction-to-opioids-heroin-prescription-drug-abuse.

Chapter 3

Rescued and Raised

"The Lord was with Joseph, and he became a successful man;
...the Lord caused all that he did to prosper in his hands.
So Joseph found favor in his sight..."

Genesis 39:2-4 (NKJV)

Joseph found himself in Egypt, sold into slavery, far from the destiny he thought God had for him. Yet, God was with Joseph, and he was raised out of the pit, from slavery to head of his master's house. There were times when I thought I would never escape the hold of drug addiction. Yet God had a plan for my life. I was rescued from the darkness and exalted to blessings I thought I would never see. I became a prominent leader for the faith and was greeted with success in all I endeavored.

"It's been a long comeback. Things were pretty dark for me. But I have faith now, and it saves my day. I was angry with God for a long time because I was unhappy with myself. I hadn't learned to make the distinction between God and my parents. But there's a peace now. In the end, I got sick and tired of being sick and tired."

-William Hurt

After several years of battling with drug addiction, I got tired of fighting, and I wasn't doing a good job on my own. I was seeing others die left and right while I got high. It wasn't until I had a near-death experience that I realized that if I kept going at this rate, I would be next to die and no one could find me. All I could picture was the day my mother cried at the door. Even though I knew she had changed the locks, I knew she hadn't locked me out of her heart. I remembered her words, "You can fight this! I know you can, but you have to want to."

I knew that if I wanted to get clean, I had to return home like the parable of the rich fool. That day I had a rational thought, I had $40 to my name. Instead of using my last few dollars to buy drugs, I used it to purchase a bus ticket home. It was a few days' journey to find my way back home. The day I made it home, I crawled to the door and cried. No one was home, so I stayed there for a few hours. It was better than being in the crack house. At least at my parent's door, if I were to die, they would find me.

I had cried myself to sleep until I heard my father's voice.

"Son, is that you?" My father asked. Wondering if he was dreaming.

I looked up, barely recognizable as I had lost so much weight, my mom ran to my side and hugged me.

"Now hold up. Your mother told you already that we were not letting you back in the house on them drugs." My father said. My mother leaned back and looked into my eyes. She could tell that I was hurt. She could tell that I was broken.

"I. I, I want to be clean," I spoke. My father helped me up, and they let me in. My mother called around and found a center that would take me that day. My mother made a few more phone calls before we left. My mother, Grandmother Rosa Mae, and Ms. Betty helped pay for my recovery. Words cannot express the gratitude I have for them. My treatment was hard, but it was necessary for me to change my life around. I was the person who could always get what I wanted. So, as long as I desired drugs in my life, I would make it happen. The withdrawal symptoms were unbearable, but I knew I had some people praying for me.

The treatment helped me explore the various circumstances that led me to turn to drugs. It helped me to deal with those issues so I would no longer need to seek drugs to self-medicate. I began facing my problems and inner demons rather than running away from them. I realized that the war was within myself, and I had to overcome my inner demons and find my faith once again.

Before I became lost in drug addiction, I had these vivid dreams. I was around 16 years of age when they started. I would dream that someone kept calling my name. I would wake up drenched in sweat in the middle of the night looking to see who was in the room, only to find no one there. These dreams bothered me so much that I asked my grandfather for his advice. He told me to respond to those voices by saying, "Here I am, Here I am."

God was calling me to greatness, calling out to me to save me from the destructive path the devil had planned for me. Yet, I ignored God's call. I was running away when I should have been running towards God. When I became entrenched in drugs, the dreams subsided.

After completing drug rehabilitation, I was confused, unsure of what to do with my life. I struggled with shame because of my drug history. I thought that I felt I was the only person who had gone through the obstacles I had overcome. My father was a man of God, yet I was a former drug addicted.

Over 10 years had passed, after being in and out of jail, since I had one of those dreams again. I last heard God call me, in the quiet of my room, at night. I was 27 years old, and I responded, "Here I am, Here I am." That moment was my Saul on the road to Damascus moment, meaning that was the moment that God had changed my life.

I followed my superior divine meaning. I wanted more of God and wanted to please him every opportunity I had. It was by the grace of God that my life was saved. I allowed God to lead me on this new path, which I met two incredible women. They were respectively the director and assistant director of DFCS (Division of Family and Children Services). They saw potential in me and gave me an opportunity at a fresh start in life. They hired me as a community service developer. While working with DFCS, it blessed me to work under an amazing supervisor and an all-around amazing woman.

Our bond was real and to this day, I consider her the God-Grandmother of my children.

After running from my destiny for so long, I was back on the narrow path of salvation. Listening to God and being obedient granted me opportunities, I wouldn't have imagined a few years ago. I continued my education and graduated from Harrington University, earning my Master's and Doctorate degree in Christian education and divinity. I was still on probation, but I found divine favor.

I explained to my probation officer the vision I had for my life in ministry. He gave me his blessing and wrote a letter to the courts on my behalf. As a result, charges were commuted, and I was removed off of Georgia state probation before the State Board of Pardon and Parole and my rights restored. My criminal history was behind me, and I never looked back. God worked miracles out in my favor, and all it took was "Yes Lord, here I am. Use me."

My desires of becoming a leader like my father and grandfather were coming back. It initially started after I preached my first sermon with a captive audience of only two people. I will never forget my subject that day, "The Showdown on Mount Carmel."

I continued to study the word of God, and after some time, decided I was ready to announce my calling to the ministry I was in. I went and sat on the front row as it was custom. When addressed by the pastor of the church, I confessed to him and the church that I had been called to preach the gospel. The congregation consisted primarily of my family members and friends. They were all excited to witness me accept the mantle to carry God's word.

But what I did not fully understand at the time was that there was more to becoming a preacher than wanting to. A preacher is called, and with that calling comes trials and tribulations as the devil attacks you and the Lord refines you. It is those trials and tribulations that reveal your purpose, as God anoints you with the spirit. As a fourth-generation preacher, I witnessed the process and sacrifices made by the fore-preachers in my family as they pursued God's call. Later, I would learn first-hand the true cost of being in ministry.

After having me wait three long months, the reverend called me for a meeting. Several of my family members attended the meeting, including my parents and grandmother Rosa Mae. The reverend announced that he believed I had not been called to preach and that he would not allow me to come to his pulpit for any reason at all. I felt betrayed by my own pastor, a man of God, who stood before me and judged me by his own standard.

We all sat there in silence for a few minutes, which felt like hours. There was so much tension in the room it was hard to breathe. My parents and grandparents were furious. My facial expression was one of hurt. Other than my parents and grandparents, no one spoke up for me. I left that day with my spirit crushed. I felt as if I had failed my parents. I had failed God. The reverend's decision caused uprooting of the founding families of the ministry. The devil used him to try to prevent me from my destiny, just like he used Judas to betray Jesus.

But we know that in the end, it was Judas'
betrayal that allowed the salvation of many. What the
devil had intended for destruction, God used to fulfill his
plan. The reverend's decision to disallow me from
preaching in the ministry, his attempt to keep me from
God's calling, ended up being the best thing that could
have happened. I will never forget when my grandfather
looked me in the eye and told me he was not going to
allow someone's decision to stop me from doing what he
knew God had called me to do. No one could tell me
God was not on my side.

I left the church, but I continued to serve God
under the leadership of my father and grandfather. Not
too long after that incident, I was licensed as a pastor by
my very own grandfather, Bishop L.E. Ross, better
known as the "Bedrock" of the family. I earnestly
pursued God's calling over my life, which began humbly
with 40 people meeting at my home for service. The
congregation continued to grow, and we found favor in
the Lord's eyes.

One of the original member's mother was a local
pastor, that believed she saw something special in me
and allowed me to hold service at her church. I was
blessed again and granted a stable location to preach at.
They allowed me to use their church, their instruments,
and utilities for free. They were the true expression of
God's favor in my life. They provided me with a helping
hand when I was in need.

I had the vision to focus on people who no one
wanted to deal with; the broken, the ashamed, and the
overlooked. The people that were told they would never
amount to anything. The mission statement was "to
reach the souls that no one else wanted to reach." So I,

along with two other bishops, established a non-denominational ministry. I was installed as senior pastor, which I witnessed growing to over 1,000 members.

They say that when it rains, it pours, and so was my experience as God rained down blessing over my ministry. God used me mightily and gave me more than I ever envisioned. I became the president of the ministry, which would eventually consist of over 80 churches nationwide, serving approximately 100,000 members. I traveled throughout the United States, laboring before God, spreading the Gospel and uplifting His people.

Through my hard work, my members blessed me financially. On one of my pastoral anniversaries, I was gifted a custom-made Bentley with a crown symbol embroidered in the headrest, which represented the prince of the Gospel. I was shocked and overwhelmed to be showered with so much love. In addition, I was presented with a presidential edition Rolex watch as a gift for my accomplishments within the ministry.

The admiration of my obedience to God didn't stop there. I found it surreal that I was the one being recognized by some of the biggest names in the gospel world, speaking at conferences that contain upwards of 75,000 people. It was such a pleasure to be around so many devoted Christians.

The greatest moment for me was being in the room and being recognized by a man that I would consider to be the father of the Gospel. I have always looked up to him and feel he has done more than any person I know for the Gospel. I am a scholar to his work and have read a majority of his books. So, to be around a man of his caliber and to be recognized by that man, was such an honor. I am forever thankful for his encouragement, inspiration, and motivation to follow the path he has led.

Life Applications

The Bible clearly states that if you are with God, then there is nothing that can stop you. Within a short period of time I went from being a drug addict in and out of prison, with only $40 and a bus ticket, to a successful preacher leading thousands of followers. The Lord sent his angels to guide me and I straightened out my life and dedicated it to serve God.

I could have let someone's decision deter me from God's purpose for my life and missed out on God's timing but thank God I had people who saw greatness inside of me. How many of us allow someone's opinion, decision, or belief keep us from going forward in life? We all have been guilty of this one time or another but the lesson learned should be that you shouldn't let anyone or anything hold you back from your greatness. Don't let anyone dim your light, not even yourself.

Things will get hard, that's a given. As long as you have vision, no matter how many times you lose sight you can still finish the race because with vision you see past things that get in your way.

There will be times in which you feel as if even you can't do something but it is in those times in which you need to lean on your support system. If you feel as if you don't have a support system then find affirmations, scriptures, words of encouragement to keep you going in your darkest hour. No matter what comes to discourage you, don't stop. You can slow down but don't stop. Please use the affirmations, scriptures, and quotes below to help you in your darkest moments.

Affirmations:

- Great things are coming my way.
- I walk in abundance and increase in abundance.
- I am powerful and capable to reach my goals.
- I confidently triumph as a champion.
- I have what it takes to start and stay strong.

Scriptures:

- "But he said to me, 'My grace is sufficient for you, for my power is made perfect in weakness.'" (2 Corinthians 12:9 NIV)
- "The righteous cry out, and the Lord hears them; he delivers them from all their troubles. The Lord is close to the brokenhearted and saves those who are crushed in spirit." (Psalm 34:17-18 NIV)
- "We are hard pressed on every side, but not crushed; perplexed, but not in despair; persecuted, but not abandoned; struck down, but not destroyed." (2 Corinthians 4:8-9 NIV)

Quotes:

- "A problem is a chance for you to do your best." – Duke Ellington

- "Everything that is done in this world is done by hope." – Martin Luther
- "Our greatest glory is not in never falling, but in rising every time we fall." – Confucius
- "Believe in yourself! Have faith in your abilities! Without a humble but reasonable confidence in your own powers you cannot be successful or happy." – Norman Vincent Peale
- "When sore trials come upon us, it's time to deepen our faith in God, to work hard, and to serve others. Then He will heal our broken hearts. He will bestow upon us personal peace and comfort." – Russell M. Nelson

Did you know?

Research has shown that for all small businesses that started in 2014, only 56% of them made it to their fifth year, meaning that 44% of those businesses failed in their fourth year.[5] From this information we can see that starting a business was not necessarily the problem, but sticking with it was another story, even with time and money invested. Although business itself can be challenging, the same concept of sticking things out can be applied to many different situations in our life.

It's so easy to quit when situations get tough, or we start feeling some discomfort. We do it all the time, from ministry to New Year's resolutions we make to gym memberships we pay for! It can be especially painful when we've made some type of investment, whether it's financial, emotional, or spiritual. But if we can press through the temporary failure, we would more often than not find ourselves on the other side of success!

People can discourage us when they see the obstacles we face, and others may even try to count us out because they don't think we're qualified. But we have to learn that not getting it right the first time or being told no isn't an automatic sign that we're doing something wrong. Not receiving the support and acceptance we expect doesn't mean we've chosen the wrong field. Many times when we start pursuing our dreams in earnest, we'll actually find that the path to success seems to get rougher. But if we stay the course no matter how impossible it looks, we'll find out that all the rejections and setbacks we experienced were really just set-ups for our success!

5. "STARTUP STATISTICS - The Numbers You Need to Know - Small ...", n.d. Accessed August 13, 2019. https://smallbiztrends.com/2019/03/startup-statistics-small-business.html.

Chapter 4

The Tragedy

"...Joseph fled and Ran outside!"

Genesis 39:12 (NKJV)

Satan hates God's children, and more so hates those that
strive to do the Lord's work. He actively seeks to destroy
such people, to tear them down, and to end their lives.
Joseph faced calamity and fled. Though he escaped, he
was not out of the woods yet. I too faced calamity, and
barely escaped with my life, only to find that the plot of
destruction had just begun.

"There are wounds that never show on the body that are
deeper and more hurtful than anything that bleeds."
- Laurell K. Hamilton, Mistral's Kiss

God had been so good to me. I was thriving in ministry, and I found a woman that loved me and believed in the vision that God had for me. We met at church one day. She was choir director, and I just so happened to be singing in the choir that day. When my eyes locked in on her, I knew that she was the one. I watched the way she praised God and served in the ministry. She was a woman after God's own heart. During service, I sought God regarding pursuing her. I wanted to make sure that I wasn't being led by my flesh.

I felt peace in my spirit. So, when service was over, I saw her, mustered up the courage and got her number. I was excited that evening and had made plans to call her the next day. But, when I reached out and called her, the number wasn't right. I was disappointed. *Perhaps, I wrote the number down wrong,* I thought.

There was a choir event coming soon, and I would be certain to see her again. Sure enough, I did. That evening led to a year and a half of dating and eventually marriage. We had a huge wedding with all of our family and friends in attendance. It was a rough 18 months of dating because her family didn't approve of me, but she didn't let that phase her.

After the wedding, we settled down into a new neighborhood in Macon, Georgia, and started a family. It was something we talked about while dating, and to see it come to fruition, my heart was full. My children were such a blessing from God. I always wanted to be a family man to give my children the love and affection I always wanted.

She stood by my side while I preached. She was a great supporter of the ministry. She would sit on the front row with the children and praise God. Not only was she active in the ministry, but she was an amazing mother and a loving wife. I was blessed to have found her.

It was a Saturday afternoon, in Macon, Georgia, when I was home with my wife and son preparing for my Sunday morning message. Typically, we would go out to eat, but that day, my wife made my favorite, grilled tilapia, and ribeye steak. I loved it when my wife cooked. She could throw down and make everything how I liked it. I was finishing up my message when my wife told me dinner would be done shortly.

It was a custom that when we ate dinner at home, we sat at the dinner table. No television, no phones, just us. It was a time that we could catch up on the week. I wanted to be as active in my children's lives as possible to ensure that they wouldn't follow in my footsteps.

After dinner, I told my wife I needed to go to the church to get some things before tomorrow. She told me to hurry back because it was getting late. I kissed her before I left and headed out. Upon entering the church, it was hot. If you're from the south, you know how hot it can get so I turned on the air condition inside the church so it would be cool for Sunday service. I grabbed a few things from my office and headed back home.

Later that night, I had an eerie feeling, but I could not identify why or where it was coming from. My

wife saw the concerned expression on my face and asked
me what was wrong. I told her that everything was all
right and explained the weird feeling that I had. We
brushed it off, said our prayers for the night, and went to
sleep.

I woke up in the middle of the night, still feeling
odd and very dehydrated. I went into the kitchen and had
a glass of water, prayed, and returned to sleep. I woke
up, the next morning, refreshed and glad that the eerie
feeling had passed. I was still unsure where the feeling
had come from.

The family and I got dressed and headed to
church. I was ready to do God's work and preach the
word. As custom before any service, someone from the
intercessory team or an elder would pray for the service
and that God's presence would be in the place.

The praise and worship that Sunday was terrific.
Everyone was up on their feet, lifting their hands and
giving God the glory. God's presence was definitely
there. The Holy Spirit was moving during worship. I
entered the pulpit and began delivering the word of God.
During my sermon, I noticed more and more people
were looking at the ceiling. I looked at the ceiling, and
something was wrong. Dust and small debris were
falling from the roof. I immediately stopped the sermon
and instructed everyone to please exit the building.

People were panicking and started pushing. I
instructed everyone to exit in a civil matter, but no one
listened as everyone was concerned for their own safety.
Everyone quickly cleared the building. I looked for my

wife and was relieved when I saw her, but was perplexed when we couldn't find our kids.

I heard a gentleman yelling for his children. My heart stopped. We soon realized that our children were still in the church. Someone yelled that they last saw our children on the back row. You could hear noises coming from the structure of the building. My adrenaline began rushing. We ran into the church with no regards for our lives. What mattered was saving our children. We couldn't dare wait on help to arrive. Time was of the essence.

We ran in and saw them on the back row. Even in all that commotion, they were sleeping. We grabbed our children and hurried out. My son was startled by what was going on and began to cry. I calmed him and told him that daddy had him. As soon as we were a mere foot outside the sanctuary, we heard a loud boom.

God's divine protection was surely with us that day because the roof of the ceiling collapsed just as we exited the church doors. We had made it out in the nick of time. I was scared and shaken, but thank the Lord that, by his grace, not one person died or was injured. Even though the church building had collapsed, we had church in that parking lot. Tears were shed by some as they hugged others. Children, including my own, clung to their parents. The building had fallen—but the true church—the ministry, was alive and whole.

Life Applications

Sometimes we ignore our inner intuition or that thought that keeps coming. We dismiss it and pay it no mind but is it trying to tell us something? I challenge you to pray that you will become sensitive to the spirit of God. God speaks daily, but we can get so busy and bogged down with life that we can't hear from God.

God doesn't just speak to us in "hunches" and through our intuition. He speaks to us in many ways. The first one being the word of God. 2 Timothy 3:16 says that all Scripture is "God-breathed." His word sometimes gives us a warning, a word of encouragement, or a lesson for life. It's "His-story"–written with love as God's guide for our lives. When was the last time you read the Bible or sat down to study his word? You could miss out on valuable information. If you think the Bible is "too old" and has a language too hard to read, try the ERV (Easy to Read Version), NIV (New International Version), or NKJV (New King James Version).

Another way God speaks is through other people. He can use a loved one, friends, teacher, or a complete stranger to relay his message to us. Their words can be a warning of what's coming, a blessing, or as a prophetic truth about our lives. What we do with the word once given, is up to us. If you're not sure if the word is from God, ask yourself these questions; Do their words line up with Scripture? Is there peace about what they said or are you uneasy?

You may think this isn't how you "hear God's voice," but it's possible that you have reduced God to your own image because He isn't acting or reacting in the way you have imagined. God is bigger than our imaginations. If you were to read Numbers 22:28, you see that He once spoke through a donkey. If he used a donkey, why then, can't He speak through anyone He chooses?

He can also speak through circumstances. He can use certain events to get our attention. Perhaps he spoke before, but you ignored his word and the people he sent to tell you. He can use circumstances to not only get our attention, but to confirm his word. God desires a relationship with us, and that includes communication. God is speaking, but are we listening?

Did you know?

Between 1989 to 2000, a research study found that the number of failed buildings, both residential and commercial, was steadily on the rise.[6] With more recent building failures in the news such as the Grenfell Tower fire in London in 2017, it's important to take care in how we build, renovate, and maintain our properties. The easy way to do things isn't always the right way to do things, and if we're not careful, it can show up in ways we least expect. Sometimes, it can literally be the difference between life and death.

In fact, much that we need to know about maintaining a structurally sound building is readily available to us in the form of assessors, inspectors, and even the Internet, if we look. But even with all this public knowledge, it's a wonder that many people and organizations don't take time to regularly inspect, maintain, and insure their buildings. It may seem like a small and even unnecessary step, but statistics and stories paint the true picture of just how important it is. If we're willing to make an investment into something that serves so many people, whether it's our home or our church; then we should also be willing to protect it.

6. "[Ebook]. Study of Recent Building Failures in the United States", n.d. Accessed August 13,2019.https://pdfs.semanticscholar.org/9e66/485748af29ac28f18234ada60d7126b9abb6.pdf.

Chapter 5

The Devil's Pawns

"When she saw that he had left his garment in her hand and had fled outside, she called out to the members of her household."

Genesis 39:13-14

Joseph escaped the temptation of Potiphar's wife, but the devil was still after Joseph. Potiphar's wife became the devil's pawn and she came up with a plan to ruin Joseph. She was going to cry out and accuse Joseph of rape. In my story, Potiphar's wife, the devil's pawn, is the greedy lender.

"It takes 20 years to build a reputation and five minutes to ruin it. If you think about that, you will do things differently."

-Warren Buffett

The church had filed a property damage claim with the insurance company. An investigation revealed a structural flaw in the church that had resulted in the roof collapsing. The insurance company agreed to pay $389,000.00 for the property damage at Rocky Creek Road.

At the time that the insurance claim was filed, the church had a bank loan for another property, Bethesda. This loan was separate from the Rocky Creek Road property. The lender filed a claim on the church that was owned free and clear with no lien. The lender had no legal interest on the damaged property, according to the terms of its mortgage (See Appendix A).

After learning about the accident at the Rocky Creek Road property and the insurance claim, the lender decided that they wanted the insurance money. Even though the lender did not cover the Rocky Creek Road property, the vice president of the lending company contacted the insurance company and requested that the lender be made the payee on the insurance claim. The lender provided documentation showing that it had issued a loan to the church as evidence of their alleged interest. However, what was not disclosed was that the documentation provided only applied to the Bethesda property, not the property on Rocky Creek Road.

To simplify the situation, I will use an analogy. Imagine you have two cars, a Honda and a Toyota. You've finished making payments on the Honda, and no longer have a loan on the Honda. You still have car payments to make on the Toyota. You are making all your payments on the Toyota in full and on time every month. One day, a tree falls on the Honda, so you make an insurance claim, and the insurance company agrees to give you $10,000.

Then, the Toyota dealership decides that since they have a loan with you for the Toyota car, they want the $10,000 from the insurance on the Honda, even though the loan on the Toyota has nothing to do with the Honda. If a dealership tried to do this to you, it would outrage you. Well, this is precisely what the lender did. They put a claim to receive money that they had no legal right to receive.

Now, the insurance company should have verified that the lender had a legal right to receive funds for the Rocky Creek Road property. However, the insurance company did not do their due diligence and issued a check in the amount of $389,000 payable jointly to the church and the lender. Because the lender was not legally entitled to any portion of the insurance proceeds, the church solely provided its endorsement on the back of the insurance claim check and deposited the check in its bank account in August 2005.

On September 19, 2005, an attorney on behalf of the lender sent a letter to the church demanding that we turn over the insurance proceeds to them. We refused to do so because the lender had no right to that money. At that point, the lender threatened to call the loan, on the Bethesda property, in default and sue the church. Also, the lender instructed their attorney to quick claim the Rocky Creek Property to them without the church's knowledge or consent. This is mortgage fraud (See Appendix B).

The lender ultimately filed a claim of loss with our bank, wrongly accusing the church of forging the lender's endorsement on the insurance check. As was previously stated, there was only one signature endorsing the check when it was deposited in our bank. However, when a copy of the check was later produced, there was an apparent endorsement by the lender. None of us at the church forged the lender's signature. There was only one other party that handled that check, our bank.

It is more than likely that the man that received the check from church that day, the acting vice president, added a forged signature so that the check would go through. He would later be fired from his position at the bank and refuse a handwriting analysis to determine if he was the one that forged the signature.

His behavior was very suspicious. Not only did the bank add the endorsement of the lender, but they also failed to do their due diligence and verify the facts that were being falsely represented by the lender. As a result, the bank responded to the lender's demand and paid them $389,000 in late January 2006. Then, the bank filed a claim for the loss with their insurance company. It is important to note that the bank would later fail in 2009 and be sued by the F.D.I.C for negligence and unlawful banking practices.

Although the lender received $389,000 from the bank, they initiated legal proceeds against the church, including a suit for specific performance and foreclosure proceedings in February 2006. The lender stated that the reason for the default was the church's failure to turn over the insurance proceeds to them. However, placing the property in foreclosure was not legally possible because the lender had no legal right to the insurance proceeds, and they were well aware of this. The church had never missed one payment with them.

The church decided the best course of action was to end the foreclosure proceedings and discontinue the loan with the lender by paying them off, while obtaining new financing elsewhere. The lender claimed that the remaining balance due was $476,622.29. We were not aware that the lender had already received $389,000 from the bank. Thus, the lender was misrepresenting the payoff amount by not taking into account the insurance money they already received. The church paid the lender $476,622.29 based on what the lender said was due. So, the lender received in total $865,622.29, when they were only owed $476,622.29.

The lender filed a criminal complaint against the church, with the district attorney office knowing that they did not have a legal right to the insurance proceeds for Rocky Creek Road. The lender's lawyer had advised them, months earlier, that they did not have a perfected lien on Rocky Creek Road property. With all the lies, errors, and mistakes that the lender had made, they recognized their exposure and need to cover themselves. This is why they quickly claimed the Rocky Creek Road property after they received the $389,000 from our bank, without informing the church, our insurance company, or the district attorney. This is also why they brought criminal charges against myself and the church. They wanted to cover up their own mess ups.

Of course, the bank had to cover themselves. An attorney submitted a letter on behalf of the bank to the state prosecutor at the district attorney's office. His letter stated that the bank was the victim of fraud. He specifically named me as the individual that forged the lender's signature on the check. In addition, the bank would later claim that their security cameras were not working the day the church deposited the check.

Unbeknownst to me as to what was going on, I continued to do what I did best; spread the word of God and uplift his people, across the United States. I never thought for a moment that I, or anyone in my church, had done anything wrong or illegal. So, I kept moving, and I kept praising.

Over the two years that passed after the roof collapsed, I considered myself truly blessed. I had a beautiful family; I was doing God's work in the world, and my church continued to grow. However, I did not realize that I was going against the devil himself, and he had already placed his pawns in my world, to do his work. The storm was not behind me; it was about to begin. The government decided that somebody had to take the fall. Although I had done nothing wrong, a thriving black minister who overcame a history of drug use and juvenile convictions had become the target.

Life Applications

In business—including the church—make sure you have documented procedures and systems in place. Having these two things will help alleviate uncertainty. They also help provide consistency so that no matter who the person is, the company can deliver the same result. Think of fast-food franchises, how the food in one state is the exact same quality in another state. However, having procedures and systems will not prevent someone from doing their own thing— because it didn't stop someone from forging their signature on the check. Though it should be documented as to what will happen if someone doesn't follow the procedures.

I'm sure there was a documented procedure with the bank on how to handle checks that have two names but only one signature. I am confident that forging a signature was not part of it and had someone abided by protocol, perhaps there would have been many issues avoided. However, someone did not follow protocol or do their due diligence, as would explain why the suspected forger was fired and then refused to provide a handwriting analysis to prove his innocence.

Always, always, always get things in writing and have the documentation backed up or saved in a secure spot. It's essential that communication is clear and understood. Make copies, take pictures of the official documentation, and place it in a safe place. It's best to hold on to essential documents for life but at least seven years.

It's vital that you are a person of integrity because your name is a stake. Proverbs 22:1 (NIV) states, "A good name is more desirable than great riches; to be esteemed is better than silver or gold." It's important that you do things right and do right by people because if you are someone that lacks integrity your name will have a bad connotation to it and no one will want to be associated with you; no matter how much money you may possess.

Don't allow greed to get the best of you. There will always be the temptation for more money, more wealth and riches, and more power, but at what cost? Mark 8:36 states, "What good is it for a man to gain the whole world, yet give up his soul?" What good would it do you to gain all these things and then lose your soul and not have inner peace? Judas betrayed Jesus for 30 pieces of silver which are estimated to be—because the data isn't precise—$90 to $3,000 in today's time. Even after receiving that money, he felt guilty because he had lied, he went out and hung himself.

Don't allow greed to sway you. Always do what is right. It's better to be at peace with making the right decision than to have a lifetime of regret over making the wrong decision.

Did you know?

Predatory mortgage lending has been in the news in recent decades more often than we'd probably like to see. Just in 2012, the Department of Justice ruled against Wells Fargo for giving out loans discriminatorily to qualified borrowers.[7] It was documented that they intentionally issued subprime loans to African-American and Hispanic borrowers, even though they were just as qualified as white borrowers. This was a discovery that was shocking to many, especially coming from a bank of such longstanding and high status in the public eye.

It's sad to realize that every bank isn't automatically to be considered trustworthy just because they are financial institutions. After all, many of us have been taught as children growing up into young adulthood that banks are the place you go to not just to open a bank account, but to do business in life. From buying houses and cars to getting loans for school and personal emergencies, banks are seen as the number one ideal resource, and many times they are!

But we really have to learn to discern properly what makes good financial sense instead of just blindly trusting anyone who will give us the number we want to hear. Weighing options carefully is a responsibility many people aren't taught, and we need to learn how to do it so that we won't be taken advantage of by lenders who aren't looking out for their borrowers' best interest. This most recent housing bubble crisis showed the lack of responsibility and accountability on both sides of the equation, the lender and the average borrower. We the people have the power to avoid such disaster again by learning and staying educated about the ins and outs of our financial affairs.

7. "Justice Department Reaches Settlement With Wells Fargo Resulting ...", n.d. Accessed August 13, 2019. https://www.justice.gov/opa/pr/justice-depar tment-reaches-settlement-wells-fargo-resulti ng-more-175-million-relief.

Chapter 6

Falsely Accused

"…She called to the men of her house and spoke to them, saying, 'Sec, he has brought in to us a Hebrew to mock us. He came in to me to lie with me, and I cried out with a loud voice. And it happened, when he heard that I lifted my voice and cried out, he left his garment with me, and fled and went outside.'".

Genesis 39:14-15 (NKJV)

Joseph was blameless and blessed in his endeavors, yet he stood falsely accused by his master's wife of rape. She had no real evidence against him. The garment she held, by itself, truly had no meaning. But she used his race and his past to condemn him. He was a Hebrew among Egyptians, she cried, a slave. Who would argue against her? With nothing but the word of an evil woman, the success Joseph was blessed with, his status, and his reputation were compromised. I too found myself falsely accused, standing before a judge. The only evidence against me was the word of the bank. But like Joseph, my race and my past would be used to accuse me. Here was the bank, the lender, and myself; a wealthy black male with a criminal history. Those who heard the cry of the lender assumed surely that my gains were ill-gotten. The fact that I had turned my life around,

achieved success honestly, and was blessed by the Lord
financially was seemingly incomprehensible to those
who believed the false accusations against me. In one
day, my world and all I had accomplished was shattered.

"When one person makes an accusation, check to be sure
he himself is not the guilty one. Sometimes it is those
whose case is weak who makes the most clamour."
-Piers Anthony

On August 29, 2007, I was just returning home from a
long, exhausting ministry trip. It was past midnight and I
did not want to wake my wife. So, I went to sleep in our
guest bedroom. No one knew I was home. In the early
hours of dawn that morning, my wife answered a loud

knock on the door. She opened the door and saw about 50 federal agents armed with shotguns, rifles, and wearing bulletproof vests. My wife was terrified.

She thought they had the wrong house until they asked for me. My wife, not knowing I had returned home, told them I was not there. All the while, I was sleeping like a baby in the guest room, not hearing the commotion at the doorway of the house. She asked why they were there to arrest me, but they would not tell her. They berated my wife and demanded that she let them in the house. My wife refused. She panicked as she was concerned for the safety of the children. The agents continued to demand entry and told my wife they would get a warrant if she did not comply. She continued to refuse, and they eventually retreated to the street to place phone calls, likely to obtain a warrant.

Suddenly, I was jolted awake by the sounds of my wife yelling and screaming in a state of hysteria. She was rumbling through the house, making sure our children were okay and trying to call me on the telephone. I stepped out of the guest room and asked my wife what was going on. She was so apprehensive, she could barely talk. She told me about the federal agents outside, and she was now even more terrified because she had told the agents
I was not home.

I looked outside the curtains to see for myself only to verify the flood of federal agents and vehicles that surrounded my house. It was such an imposing presence in my small neighborhood that my neighbors were coming outside of their homes thinking someone had been murdered. From what I saw outside my home, I thought I must have made the America's Most Wanted list, and I had no idea how or why they were there for me. Although I had been arrested before in my juvenile years, I had never been in any situation like this.

I was in a state of shock. I had no idea what to do. I called my godfather, told him the details, and asked him what to do. He was very concerned, and told me to calm down and call the lawyer. I first reached out to a close friend, Mr. Kend, who was a fraternity brother of mine and an attorney. Mr. Kend told me to confirm who was at my residence. After I repeatedly told him that federal agents had surrounded my house, he said, "My brother, I honestly would like to help you, but I can't involve myself in that." I hung up, immensely frustrated. This was someone I considered to be family, and he had just recently come back from a lavish trip that was paid at my expense.

I called the attorney who had previously worked with our church. Initially I did not get an answer, but she returned my call within minutes. The first thing she said to me was, "Where are you, Sir O?" With a worried tone I told her, "I am at my house, surrounded by 50 federal agents like I'm an American gangster. What should I do?"

She replied, "Do not go to the door, let me make a phone call." I do not know who she called, but as I watched through the curtains, I saw the federal agents leaving. Still, that did nothing to ease the fear and paranoia taking over my mind.

When the attorney called me back, I answered immediately. Rapidly speaking, she said, "Do you have somewhere you can go? Pack a bag, do not use your phone, and get out of town for a while. I'll be in contact with you. Give me some time to see what evidence they have on you. Do not call any family members or church members." Something about her advice did not feel right. So, I called the bishop, the pastor, and Mrs. Davis, asking them to come over to my house right away for an urgent meeting.

Once they arrived, I told them everything that had just taken place. I told them the advice I received about leaving town until the attorney could figure out what evidence they had against me. Everyone was shocked by the news. We decided to do what any Christian would do. We prayed. We asked God for his guidance and placed the earthshaking events of the day in his Holy Hands.

After we prayed, Mrs. Davis said, "God is with you son. We're not going to run away from this. We are going to put our trust in the Lord."

At that moment, the phone rang. It was the attorney and she had decided to change the plan. She explained to me that she thought skipping town would be a bad idea and told me to meet me at her office. *Now, who can tell me that was a coincidence?* God, in his goodness, had spoken through Mrs. Davis that day. I thanked everyone for praying with me in my hour of need and coming to my home when I needed them the most. They only asked to be kept informed of what was going on.

I drove over to the attorney's office. Once I got there, the attorney revealed the indictment the federal government had on me. I was dumbfounded. I was being charged with bank fraud, money laundering, and fraud, all stemming from the events that had transpired after the roof of the church collapsed. I thought the whole ordeal was resolved following the civil suit after the church paid the lender the full balance due on the loan to avoid any further litigation. I never thought I would be accused, let alone charged of any wrongdoing.

The attorney made arrangements for me to turn myself in. We went in her vehicle to the federal courthouse. Entering the courtroom was surreal. It could have easily been a large art museum. The magistrate judge read me my charges, 72 counts of bank fraud, money laundering, and forfeiture. I entered a plea of not guilty, and I was released from custody on a $25,000 secured bond.

The judge placed me on pre-trial release, instructed that I was not allowed to leave the state of Georgia, and I was not allowed to remove my name from any church accounts. Also, peculiarly, I was not permitted to change my attorney and would have to be represented by Mrs. Gomez throughout the entire federal procedures. While on pre-trial release, my probation officer was an amazing person and very understanding. He gave me permission to travel throughout Georgia to continue preaching. I continued in my ministry, spreading the Gospel.

The thunder, lightning, and rain became a tornado. The attorney called a meeting with the leaders of the church and me. She informed us the prosecutor was not offering me a deal. We would need to prepare for trial. The attorney held another meeting with all the church members who were scheduled to appear before the jury to testify.

She gave them legal advice on how to respond to the questions of the U.S. Prosecutor. Although she was a competent attorney, she should have presented all the legal advice she gave to myself and church members to the court and removed herself from the case. Mrs. Gomez was the same attorney who fought the civil suit that was brought against us by our lender.

This is what is considered a conflict of interest, and so, the attorney should not have been my criminal defense attorney for this related case. Had I known that at the time, she would not have been my criminal attorney. The false accusations brought against me were in the news and media, tarnishing my reputation as a man and pastor. I was determined to clear my name. I was sure truth and justice would prevail. I was going to trial.

Life Applications

When situations seem to be spiraling out of control, it's easy to go with the first hasty solution that makes sense. It also seems natural to defer to those who are qualified in areas we're not, or to take advice from a source that's more knowledgeable than we are. Yet, God is the ultimate source of knowledge and wisdom, and he knows what to do in any situation.

Isaiah 55:8 says, "'For my thoughts are not your thoughts, nor are your ways my ways,' says the Lord." Since God always knows better, we have to make an effort to not be led by our emotions, the emotions of others, or the severity of a situation. Instead, we need to pause if we feel like we're about to make a choice that doesn't sit right, turn to God, and ask him what to do.

While we are considering what to do in stressful situations, the good thing is we don't have to figure everything out by ourselves! Many of us have family, friends, co-workers, spouses, bosses, mentors, and more. When we don't know what to do, or we're not completely sure, we can find assurance in the words of those who we know only to have the best in mind for us. This is laid out in Proverbs 11:14, "Where *there is* no counsel, the people fall; But in the multitude of counselors, *there is* safety."

If we make decisions without asking for input and opinions from others we trust, we can be setting ourselves up for failure. But when we weigh our decisions with the wisdom of others, we can be reassured that the resolution we've come up with is one that is proven and will hold up under pressure. There will be a peace that comes with it.

Difficult circumstances will come, no matter how good life seems to be going. It's up to us to handle them properly, no matter what is being said about us or how terrifying it seems. This is accomplished by seeking God and getting wise counsel from others before we choose our next steps.

Did you know?

It's a news story we hear that makes our stomach drop while our heart leaps: another man or woman who was convicted of a crime they didn't commit is finally exonerated years later. The stories we hear of the time lost with their families or their future and dreams being stolen are absolutely heart-wrenching. Unfortunately (and fortunately), it's a story that has become more and more prevalent in recent years. It's fortunate because justice is finally being served. But it's unfortunate that these convictions have happened in the first place.

As of August 13, 2019, The National Registry of Exonerations project reports that there have been 2,480 exonerations since 1989, with a total of 21,891 years of time lost by the wrongfully convicted.[8] According to this same registry, there has been a marked increase in the number of exonerations performed starting in 2012 onward. This information points us to the idea that there may be more people who are falsely convicted of a crime and imprisoned than we have previously thought.

It's easy to assume that justice is always served correctly, especially in a country where the criminal justice system is so extensive and complex. But in the case of the many exonerated and those whose stories are yet to be told truthfully, they and their families know otherwise. We have to know that if a wrongful conviction has been served, we have the power to appeal. Our justice system has evolved so that we no longer have to accept a faulty judgment that can alter the course of our lives and damage our reputation for years. We can fight for justice, confident in knowing that the truth will prevail.

8. "Exonerations in the United States Map", n.d. Accessed August 14, 2019. https://www.law.umich.edu/special/exonerat ion/Pages/Exonerations-in-the-United-States -Map.aspx.

Chapter 7

The Trial

"So it was, when his master heard the words which his
wife spoke to him, saying, "Your servant did to me after
this manner," that his anger was aroused. Then Joseph's
master took him and put him into the prison, a place
where the king's prisoners *were* confined. And he was
there in the prison."

Genesis 39:19-20 (NKJV)

One can assume that Joseph attempted to plead his case,
to claim his innocence, but Potiphar, the master, was
already blinded and enraged by the lies of his wife.
Joseph was unceremoniously thrown in prison. I was
determined to have my day in court, for the truth to
vindicate me. But the deck was already stacked against
me. We are taught that the judicial system is one in
which justice prevails, but I would find that our judicial
system, in reality, is one in which those in power can
push their own agenda. Like Potiphar, the jury was
blinded by deceit and trickery, and even denied
clarification when they sought it.

"You have to realize that myself and others that have
been wrongfully convicted of crimes, we've dealt with
the situation. You realize that you're not going to
survive in prison or progress as a human being if you
allow yourself to continue in this negative energy."

-Brian Banks

The trial commenced on March 3, 2008. During my trial, my attorney, the people of the ministry, and I strived to prove my innocence. First, an executive board of the ministry took the stand. He testified that he, not myself, endorsed the insurance check on behalf of the church. He testified that I did not participate in any fashion with the depositing of the check and I never touched nor signed the insurance check. He also testified that I never asked anyone to endorse the name of the lender on the insurance check.

Next to take the stand was a forensic documents examiner and handwriting identification expert, certified by the American Board of Forensic Document Examiners. He was formerly a special agent with the United States Army Criminal Investigation Division. He examined the endorsements on the $389,000 check, and he examined the handwriting and signatures of myself, ministry members, and employees. He testified that the executive board member signed the ministry's endorsement on the back of the check. The forensic documents examiner testified that it is highly probable in his expert analysis that the lender's endorsement was not signed by myself, or by the ministry members. Thus, the lender's endorsement was signed by someone outside the ministry.

Next to testify was the employee of the bank that received the $389,000 check. The employee was fired from the bank for failing to follow protocol and for not verifying the signatures on the back of the check when he received it. On the witness stand, he was evasive. He refused to submit to a handwriting analysis by experts that would have discerned if he was the one to endorse the lender's signature on the check. When asked in the courtroom, "why he refused the expert handwriting analysis", he had no answer. When asked if the lender's endorsement was on the check when he received it, he said he did not remember.

A member of the ministry, employed in the construction business, testified that the insurance money was used for the purpose intended. The money was used to replace the building with the collapsed roof. The prosecution painted me as a deviant and criminal mastermind. They pointed out the car I drove and the house I lived in as evidence of my criminal lifestyle, even though the money used to purchase those things had nothing to do with the insurance money. They pointed to my juvenile criminal history, even though I had turned my life around to serve God.

The prosecutor told the jury that I had moved the money out of the account. That I had "laundered" the money. However, it was testified that the transfer of the funds was authorized and ordered by the board of the ministry while I was outside the state of Georgia. The money was moved to another account to prevent the potential seizure of the funds. My attorney was inexperienced in criminal defense at the federal level. This became evident on the day of trial. Hindsight and other attorneys would later reveal that there were several critical errors my attorney made.

First, she should have removed herself as my defense to be a witness on my behalf. If she had done that, she would have been able to testify everything she did to fight the lender, as the ministry's attorney, in the civil and foreclosure suit that the lender brought against us. Second, she should have hired an insurance and mortgage expert to testify that there was no misconduct in the cashing of the check received for the damages on the church property. Also, an expert could have testified that the lender had no right to any of the funds from the insurance check. Doing so would prove that no crime was committed, and I was innocent.

For months my name and picture were all over the local media channels and newspapers with headlines "*Leader steals money from ministry*." I was eager to have that headline be, "*Leader found innocent*." I was sure the jury would see the truth and find me not guilty.

The jury deliberated for seven days. During the deliberation process, the jury sought clarification. They asked the judge, "If the defendant isn't guilty of bank fraud, does that mean he is not guilty of anything else?" To me, this was an indication that the jury felt that no bank fraud was committed. The judge should have told them that if no bank fraud was committed, then automatically, money laundering could not have occurred.

Money that is obtained honestly and legally, has no need to be laundered. Instead, the judge told the jury to re-read their jury instructions and offered no other clarification. Also, during the jury's deliberation, one of the jurors got sick. I believe that the jury was pushing for a hung jury and a mistrial. They clearly did not feel comfortable with issuing a guilty verdict. Instead, the judge replaced the juror with an alternative that did not hear any of the arguments during the trial.

After seven days, the jury reached a verdict. I stood in the courtroom, expecting to hear my name cleared, but on March 10, 2008, I was convicted on one count of bank fraud and 53 counts of money laundering. I could barely remain standing. The judge assigned my sentencing date for June 6, 2008, and adjourned the court.

Waiting to be sentenced was extremely difficult on my family and me emotionally. I did not know it then, but the last Sunday before my sentencing date would be the last service I would be a part of for a very long time. The ministry attendance was under capacity that day. Many had left the ministry after believing what they saw on the news about me. But I was still going to preach God's word to the members present, which was mainly the founding families of the ministry.

The spirit was within us all. Then, all of a sudden, a different type of anointing came over everyone. People began to weep out loud, and I could feel their pain. That Sunday I saw a side of my grandmother, that I had never seen before. She stood up and started wailing and screaming. She was usually the strongest of the family, but she lost it that day. She shouted, "The attachment is broken." I did not know what she meant at that time, but later, she revealed to me that the Lord told her I had to go to prison. That day there were so many people crying and fainting that there were not enough ushers to console them.

The day of my sentence, I was approached by nearly every Georgia media organization, being asked for an interview as I made my way to the courthouse. The whole courtroom was full to capacity with my family, friends, and ministry members. On June 6, 2008, I was sentenced to an egregious 130 months (10 years and 10 months) in prison. I was devastated. I could not comprehend how I could receive so much time for a crime I never committed. I would later learn that in the federal system, individuals that fight for their innocence receive significantly harsher sentences.

Also, black men statistically receive disproportionately longer prison sentences. It was unjust, but it was happening. I felt numb and had difficulty processing in my mind what was happening. Even if I was guilty, which I wasn't, the research I had done showed that a typical sentence for this type of crime was 10 years probation with no prison time, or at most, maybe two years in prison. Everything that I had sacrificed over the years for ministry and everything I was going to lose. flashed through my mind. I stood firm, not letting my feelings and emotions overpower my publicly professed faith in front of the people. In my mind, I was asking, "Why God?" I had to turn inward within myself to what I had been taught. and what I believed was that the man up above would bring me through this madness.

I turned to the ministry members present in the courtroom. I wanted them to put their faith not in me, not in the courts, but in God alone. I told them, "God has not brought us this far to leave us."

Lesson Learned

It's easy to say what you would do when you're not in the midst of a situation, but when you're face to face with adversity, that's when your faith is tested. When my trial date came, I was confident that I would be found not guilty, but that was not the case. All facts were not presented that could have helped exonerate me, and people manipulated information about my lifestyle to help paint me in a negative light.

But even though things did not go in my favor, I still held on to my faith in knowing that God will prevail. Forces that be, wanted me to give up hope. Even though man and the judicial system failed me, due to being corrupt. I serve a God that even though I might not understand his plan, he will never leave me or forsake me. I'm not going to lie and say that I wasn't shocked or that it didn't ever feel like I was in a bad dream, but I knew that things would eventually turn around in my favor.

I have preached hundreds of messages about trusting God. Lean not unto your own understanding, enduring persecution for the glory of God and so here was my chance to live out the very words that I have preached. Though the world tried to shame me, I stood firm on the truth. I was innocent, and though they slay me, in God, I will trust.

Did you know?

So many people turn a blind eye to the racial bias that is prominent in society. There have been notable cases that show how law enforcement has treated black men who were compliant with their instructions yet have lost their lives. And how a white man can follow a black teenager, however, claim to feel threatened when he shoots and kills the young man, and the juror finds him not guilty. Our system is prejudiced, and it is harder for African Americans to receive the same treatment and sentence for the same crime as their Caucasian counterparts. According to a survey done by Sentencingproject.org[1]

---

[1] The Sentencing Project. Criminal Justice Facts. Sentencingproject.org. https://www.sentencingproject.org/criminal-justice-facts/ (Accessed August 26, 2019)

"Sentencing policies, implicit racial bias, and socioeconomic inequality contribute to racial disparities at every level of the criminal justice system. Today, people of color makeup 37% of the U.S. population but 67% of the prison population. Overall, African Americans are more likely than white Americans to be arrested; once arrested, they are more likely to be convicted; and once convicted, they are more likely to face stiff sentences. Black men are six times as likely to be incarcerated as white men, and Hispanic men are more than twice as likely to be incarcerated as non-Hispanic white men."

Where is the justice in that? These are things that we, as a society, need to correct. I believe Benjamin Franklin had it right when he said: "Justice will not be served until those who are unaffected are as outraged as those who are."

Chapter 8

Damage and Pain

Then Joseph's master took him and put him into
the prison, a place where the king's
prisoners *were* confined. And he was there in the
prison. But the LORD was with Joseph and showed him
mercy, and He gave him favor in the sight of the keeper
of the prison.

Genesis 39:20-21 (NKJV)

Joseph was taken from his homeland, made a slave, and
then thrown in prison, though he did no wrong. His faith
was tested. I am sure he even questioned God,
wondering how God could allow all these things to
happen. I remember well the word of prophecy that was
spoken over me. It was said to me that I was going to
live everything that I ever preached. Along with Joseph,
I enjoyed the teachings of Jacob. These two biblical
figureheads both lost everything, their families, and their
possessions. I sat in jail with the same plight. I lost
family members, my home, my reputation, and I was
separated from my children. I questioned God, not
knowing if I would have the strength, like these biblical
men, to make it through. Only God's strength would
allow me to survive the damage and pain I would
endure.

"The words you speak become the house that you live
in."
-Hafiz

The damage to my life began even before I was convicted and sentenced to 130 months in prison. With the initial accusations alone, I lost my reputation. I lost my credibility as a leader of the ministry. I had turned my life around and abandoned the drugs and crime of my youth. I, along with my family, had sacrificed much so the ministry would thrive.

So, it filled me with anguish to be viewed as a swindler, a con-artist, who stole money from his own people. Often, successful leaders are stereotyped to be mass manipulators, crooked people that prey on people's faith and hope. Now, here I was, being labeled as such. I was accused of stealing money, but how could I steal from myself. I had donated and given away more money than the amount I was charged with taking.

After my indictment, I lost my father six months before my trial. He was my best friend and greatest mentor. I believe the legal accusations and scandal faced by the ministry was too much stress on him. I remember him telling me, "Son, I have already lived a good life, I want you to be able to live yours. There is not much they [the judicial system] can do to harm me." My father was willing to take my place and go to prison for me if it came to that. Like Jesus Christ, he was ready to sacrifice his own life, so that I could live mine in freedom.

My father died at the age of 64. To lose him really broke my heart. I miss him still. Two weeks after my trial, I lost my home. My house was burned down. Surely, my faith was being tested.

When the day came to turn myself in, it was only by the grace of God that I was able to get out of bed and stand up. Once I turned myself in, I was sent to Osceola, Georgia. One of the guards recognized my face, likely from all the media coverage my case had. He told me, "I can't believe the judge gave you that much time. I never saw him give anyone that much time before."

To me, he was another reminder of the injustice I was suffering. I did, however, appreciate his empathy. When the guard told me he would be praying for me, I sat in that holding facility and cried. I kept pondering how something like this could happen to a man who was doing the work of God.

From the Osceola holding facility, I was transported to the prison in Forest City, Arkansas. I was surrounded by hundreds of strangers. I was nervous and terrified. There is no manual that they give you before you go to prison that can prepare you for the lifestyle shock. I learned how the procedures worked from other inmates.

In prison, discrimination is commonplace. Who you can talk to, where you can go, and where you can sit to eat or watch TV is primarily determined by the color of your skin. Anyone that is "different" from the institutionalized "norm" is treated poorly. Men that are feminine, homosexual, or transgender, are harassed. Individuals with mixed races are not treated as well as those that are considered "pure" blood.

As a leader, I welcomed all to my ministry. In my congregation, there were people of all different races and cultures. Going to prison, where the racial tensions were high, felt like stepping back in time 60 years. It was disheartening to see the level of ignorance and animalistic behaviors displayed by some inmates. This was not the case for every person I encountered, but unfortunately, prison can take a toll on some more than others and sap away an individual's humanity.

Inmates are not the only ones to sometimes lose their humanity in prison. I encountered staff members that displayed the same level of ignorance and discrimination as the inmates. I met staff members that abused their power to bully inmates. I remember asking a staff member a question and being told, "Shut up and kiss my behind." And that was the nice version. I was shocked. Not all staff members were like this, but some were consistently disrespectful and treated inmates as less than human.

During my incarceration, I was moved to several facilities. I would serve time in Arkansas, Tennessee, Alabama, Oklahoma, Georgia, and Florida. Prison overcrowding was evident. At one location, I was placed in a 10-man cell with only one way in or out.

It was challenging to stay in touch with my family members while I was incarcerated. Family is an important support system that can help inmates get through their time. Although the Bureau of Prisons states that they support family contact, the reality is that they make it difficult to maintain regular contact with your family. When I was incarcerated far from my hometown, it was difficult for my family to see me. Phone calls were costly. I once paid $20 for one 15-minute phone call. In this digital age, their phone system is archaic. Inmates are only allowed 300 minutes of phone time every month.

This equates to 10 minutes a day, less when a month has 31 days. So, I had 10 minutes or less every day to try to speak with my wife, children, mother, and others that were dear to me. It was simply not enough. What killed me the most was knowing that my children went from a stable upper-middle-class lifestyle with both parents, to a single-parent home. I was forced to miss some of the most precious and vital years of my children's lives, and I will never be able to get those years back. In particular, my daughter was very young when I was incarcerated, and she has grown up only knowing me from a couple of hours of visitation.

After several years in prison, I was devastated with the receipt of divorce papers from my wife. We were married for over 10 years and went through a lot together. We had the same problems as any other marriage, but overall, I thought our marriage was amazing. We worked together in ministry and raised our children together. She was my backbone when I needed comfort.

Although I was deeply saddened by the divorce, I understood her decision. She wanted to hide the children from the embarrassment and shame that my conviction brought. She was unwilling to put her life on hold for nine years. After our divorce, she discontinued communication with me. Sadly, this further reduced the opportunities I had to communicate with my children. I was no longer talking to my kids regularly, and I worried that they would think that I did not care about them. In truth, I thought about them daily, and my separation from them tore my soul.

Ultimately, after being incarcerated at several different facilities, I ended up at Coleman Low Prison.

Coleman was where I did the hardest time. At that place, my faith was tested the most. I went through so many obstacles there, and I even had a few breakdowns. There was so much negativity in that place that I still need a spiritual cleanse.

While at Coleman, I lost loved ones dear to me as they passed on to be with God. One of these people was Mrs. Martha Fields. She was like a mother to me. I also lost my grandfather and was saddened that he was not able to make it two more years to see me return home.

Coleman was the last place I would see "Granny." She came to see me for my birthday. That week the prison was doing an awful job managing visitation. There were computer issues amongst the many other problems going on, and my family waited many hours to see me. Generally, at a certain point in the day, they wouldn't allow visitors to come in anymore, but God knew I needed to see her that day. With only 15 minutes remaining for visitation, the lieutenant allowed my grandmother in. Those 15 minutes would be the last I would spend with her. She died a month later.

Within two days of my grandmother's death, I lost a mentor of mine, Mr. Bertham Witham, the humanitarian of our ministry. I met him initially because Granny worked as his housekeeper before she passed. With their love, financial support, and vision to reach God's people, I was able to do some amazing things in ministry. Mr. Witham loved Granny and myself, and I will forever keep his name alive because he believed in me.

With so much pain, death, and damage happening, I became numb all over again, just like the day I was sentenced. But God was with me, he provided what I needed to make it through.

I lost everything except my soul, my faith, and a few who stood by me through the journey. Even though I was a victim of the system and damaged by the law, I will not be a victim forever. I will rise above, all the way up. In the words of my late father, "For every fall, there is a promotion," and I know mine is on the way.

Lessoned Learned

Life can be full of twists, turns, and surprises. Never would I have thought in a million years that I would have ended up in prison. During my time, I lost loved ones dear to me and damaged relationships that I never intended. We can take for granted hearing a loved one's voice on the phone, especially when you talk to them daily. But, when that privilege is taken away, you realize how vital those phone calls were to you.

It was very hurtful when my wife left, but I understood her viewpoint and reason for doing what she did. But going from a two-parent household to a single mother is not only financially stressing but emotionally damaging to the children and everyone involved. I envisioned being there for my children and encouraging them just as my father did with me. Not being in their lives to witness them grow and experience significant events with them perturbed me. Those moments I will never be able to get back.

Those years in prison stretched my faith in ways I couldn't imagine. As much as I preached about Job, I had to reflect back on how he could survive all the pain and loss. His family and friends knew he had to have done wrong and that God was punishing him. Even when people doubted Job, Job still held onto his faith. Yes, Job had a fleshly moment, but he gained back his focus and clarity.

Because he did not curse God or give up, he received a double portion for his trouble. I pray that for my heartache, loss, and faithfulness, I receive the same.

Did you know?

The divorce rate in the United States is nearly 50%, but that amount nearly doubles when there is a significant other that experiences jail time for more than one year. According to Thespruce.com,[2]

---

[2] Stritof, Sheri. Impact of a Prison Sentence on a Marriage. Thespruce.com. https://www.thespruce.com/what-is-a-prison-marriage-2300889 (Accessed August 26, 2019)

"Spouses who are left at home suffer from feelings of being an outcast, guilt, shame, loneliness, financial hardship, and sexual frustration. Phoning can be expensive. There is even stress from the visiting room procedures that many prisons impose on families. The divorce rate among couples where one spouse is incarcerated for one year or more is 80 percent for men and close to 100 percent for women. Another study found that each year of incarceration increases the odds that the inmate's marriage will end in divorce (before or after the inmate gets out of prison) by an average of 32 percent. That does not leave many couples in this situation with much hope of making their marriage work."

In an article by Emma Green, she interviewed Kelly Rath, an administrator in the Oregon Department of Corrections, working on inmate advocacy and community-building. In the article Rath states [3]

---

[3] Green, Emma. What It's Like to Be a Prison Chaplin. Theatlantic.com. August 17, 2015. Accessed August 26, 2019. https://www.theatlantic.com/national/archive/2015/08/helping-people-find-god-in-a-prison-cell/401414/

"When someone goes to prison, their life "on the outside" doesn't stop. Moms still die. New nieces and nephews still get born....When prisoners get a call from the outside, sharing news of a death,break-up, or other important life changes, their relationship with the person on the other end of the phone "is usually full of unspoken things," she said. "It may knock them out, to think that I now have to deal with the reality of why I'm here, that I too may die here.""

Having to deal with life moving on without you while you're contemplating how to survive day to day within prison is a heavy toll on any person. Besides the physical demands of surviving, one has to consider the mental turmoil and anguish that inmate endures.

Chapter 9

Federal Favor

And Joseph's master took him and put him into
the prison, the place where the king's prisoners were
confined, and he was there in prison. But the LORD was
with Joseph and showed him steadfast love and gave him
favor in the sight of the keeper of the prison. And the
keeper of the prison put Joseph in charge of all the
prisoners who were in the prison. Whatever was done
there, he was the one who did it. The keeper of the
prison paid no attention to anything that was in Joseph's
charge, because the LORD was with him. And whatever
he did, the LORD made it succeed.

Genesis 39:20-23 (ESV)

There are few things worse than being thrown in prison,
one of them is losing everything. Joseph was in prison,
but never did God abandon him. Instead, the Lord
watched over Joseph and protected him. He granted
Joseph favor with the guards and used Joseph as his
vessel to minister to other prisoners. Although there
were times when my faith was shaken, God was always
with me. The Lord watched over me and also granted me
favor. Like Joseph, I was literally charged with the care
of other inmates when transported on a bus between
institutions. There was much pain in my life, but also
much that God had to teach me. There were many people
I needed to meet for my personal journey. There were
times when God wanted to use me to minister to these
people, but also times when God placed people in my
life to minister to me.

"Don't let a temporary period of being uncomfortable keep you from a permanent blessing. Yes, it takes discipline. Yes, it's uncomfortable. But your destiny is at stake."
-Joel Osteen.

Prison is a dark place, but no darkness can keep the Lord's light from shining through. God had much to teach me while I was in prison. While I struggled, he gave me strength and showed me favor in the prison system. He used me as his vessel to reach inmates and minister to the very people I based my ministry's mission statement on, "To reach the souls no one else wanted to reach." At the same time, God placed in my path individuals that would help steer me, navigate prison, minister to me, and help me through the hardest times of my incarceration.

During the nine years I spent in prison, I was blessed to come across some great men and women. Some were inmates, and some were staff. God's favor was evident since day one when I entered the Osceola Holding Facility. In those early weeks of my sentence, I was given so much hope and prayer to keep my faith alive.

When I was transferred to Forest City, I met a man who went by the name of T.K. T.K. was the local leader (shot caller) of a known brotherhood. Typically, this brotherhood does not associate with blacks. As you can see, prison was very segregated. Although it is very unusual for an Aryan brother to speak to a black man, for some reason T.K. decided to teach me the prison basics. He made sure I was protected and gave the word to the compound that I was a man of God and not to be messed with by anyone. T.K. taught me the do's and don'ts, including where to sit and where to go. Although he was a gang leader, T.K. was a humble, genuine, and caring man, reminding me that diamonds can be indeed found in the rough. I am thankful for his help, and I believe God was also using both of us to help ease the racial tensions in that prison.

I also had the honor and pleasure to meet a popular fellow Georgia native. Although he had fame, he was extremely sincere, polite, and respectful with a great reputation as a successful music artist, actor, and writer. One day during visitation, my son recognized him and asked if he could go over and meet him. I allowed my son to go and say hello, but then I noticed that he was talking to him for a while and I did not want my son to take up too much of his family visit time.

When I walked over to get my son, I heard the artist telling him about doing the right thing. He told my son that going to prison was not something to be proud of and that he should respect the law. To see this famous person dedicating his visit time to teach my son a life lesson was a real blessing. It gave me a new outlook on life, showing me that preachers are not the only ones that can spread good news and words of wisdom. I know that today, this artist is using his influence to positively influence the lives of people headed in the wrong direction. I am thankful for his words and dedication.

I was viewed by staff as a peacekeeper. If there were tension among inmates, the administrator would ask me to bring peace. When I transferred to Coleman Prison, it was tough, but luckily, God placed people in my life to help me through. My friend Tim was always an encouragement to me. He would walk with me on the track and talk with me during tough times. Gomez is a man I met that had really turned his life around to do good in this world. I met Gomez in Atlanta Holdover Prison.

Years later we would cross paths again at Coleman. Well, as fate would have it, we got to talking at Coleman and realized that we had actually met years before either of us had gotten incarcerated. He and his family had actually attended one of the ministry's satellite locations, in Georgia. With God, there are no coincidences.

When Granny passed, I was a wreck and at the time unable to use the phone to talk to my family. Both Tim and Gomez were there for me during that difficult time. I am forever grateful.

All throughout my journey, I never stopped spreading the Gospel, praying, or worshiping our father in heaven. Near the end of my sentence, I was approached by a media group to film a documentary regarding my story and the experiences of other inmates that were changing their lives for the better. Such a documentary would have been unprecedented. Unfortunately, it was denied.

Lessoned Learned

No matter where you go, if you are a child of God, God has you. God's favor was on my life, even being in prison. I had my moments of brokenness, but prison couldn't break me. Even when society meant me harm, and people wanted to see me suffer, God made provision and provided protection.

Even amid my sentence, I still managed to minister to people. What's in you will come out, especially during hard times. It is during the hard times that people learn what they are capable of. It is when your back is against that wall that you have no other choice but to stand tall and face your fears. It is when you feel as if everyone has forsaken you when you realize that Jesus was always there.

When you're a kingdom citizen, God will always have a word for you, even if it's an unlikely source. Even in my wilderness, God sent people to encourage me and help me through some dark moments. When you are one to give peace, peace shall find you, even in the midst of unlikely places.

Did you know?

Behind those prison walls, men change. Whether that's for good or bad, the decision is left up to that person. But prison does have its way of bringing the worst out of people. Whether it's always having to watch your back, the imminent fear of your life being endangered, or the whispers of you being sexually assaulted or raped, prison can make a grown man do things he never imagined.

In an article that talks about church behind prison bars, states that

> "While it's yet to be documented how many prisoners regularly attend Christian services in America, almost 24,000 prisoners nationwide participate in Prison Fellowship classes and services every month. Set against the backdrop of multi-million dollar homes, the Carol Vance Unit in Richmond, Texas, is small and unassuming for a prison. Behind the correctional facility's gates is the Prison Fellowship's® longest-running Academy.

> Jerrel Martin has been at Carol Vance for less than two years, only entering a life of crime at 40, after his business went downhill. Until his incarceration, Martin didn't think he had much use for God, whom he blamed for the death of

his four brothers to a childhood disease. But after staring at the inside of a prison for long enough, Martin decided to stop giving God the cold shoulder.

"God put me on Earth for a purpose," he says in a strong Louisiana cadence. "A living dog is better than a dead lion. As long as you're living, there's still hope."

Today, Martin is one of the leaders of a tight-knit group of men that meets regularly for worship, teaching, discipleship, and prayer to encourage each other to grow in faith while behind bars. It's Church. Prison Church. And it's clear that God is here.""

4

---

[4] Erler, Zoe. The church behind bars: supporting Christians in prison. Prisonfellowship.org. October 4, 2017. https://www.prisonfellowship.org/2017/10/church-behind-bars-supporting-christians-in-prison/ (Accessed August 29, 2019)

People can change and even have the desire to change for better, but a lot of times, many prisoners don't know how or don't have the resources or outlets to do so. I thank God for those organizations that are actively involved within the prison to help better the lives of inmates.

Chapter 10

The Appeal

"... Make mention of me unto Pharaoh, and bring me out
of this house: For indeed I was stolen away out of the
land of the Hebrews: and here also have I done nothing
that they should put me into the dungeon."

Genesis 40:14-15 (KJV)

Joseph was an innocent man in prison. Yes, the Lord
was with Joseph and had granted him favor with the
chief jailer. Yes, God used Joseph to minister to others
in prison, but Joseph longed for freedom. He wanted to
return to his home and his family. So, he commissioned
the chief cupbearer to appeal to Pharaoh on his behalf.
Like Joseph, I was in prison for a crime I never
committed, and although God had revealed to me his
light in the darkness of places, I too desired freedom.
During my incarceration, I would continue to fight for
justice in a broken system.

"Better to die fighting for freedom then be a prisoner all
the days of your life."
-Bob Marley

During my lengthy prison sentence, I, along with others, continued to fight for my freedom and my innocence. I filed an appeal.

Americans have a right to a speedy trial, but this does not apply to the appeals process. The system is designed in such a way that it is tough for an innocent man, wrongfully convicted, to have his case reheard, or his verdict overturned. This is even more true for black men who are the least likely to ever win an appeal.

The appeal process is also costly as I would find out. I obtained new legal representation. The previous attorney submitted an affidavit to the court admitting that she was ineffective as counsel. For my appeal, my new attorney acquired an attorney that specializes in property law and title searches. In his testimony, he stated...

"It is my expert legal opinion that the Bethesda Avenue property and the Rocky Creek property [the one that collapsed] are two separate and distinct parcels of real estate, with the Rocky Creek property being situated to the south of the Bethesda Avenue property, and adjacent to the same, with no apparent overlaps in the deed descriptions. The Rocky Creek Property was at no time in the public record conveyed to the lender as security for a loan.

Based upon the foregoing documentation that I have reviewed, it is my expert legal opinion that the Rocky Creek property is free and clear of Deeds to Secure Debt or other liens and was free

and clear of any liens in May 2005 when the
roof on the building at that property collapsed.
Based upon the foregoing documentation that I
have reviewed, it is my expert legal opinion that
the lender did not have any legal interest giving
them right to any insurance proceeds on the
Rocky Creek Road property in May 2005."

The next person my new attorney acquired was an
insurance expert. He had extensive and substantive
experience relating directly to insurance applications and
policies. The insurance expert read and reviewed various
records and documents in my case. He gave his expert
opinion as to whether the loss payment check issued by
the insurance company was required to be made payable
to the lender, which the lender claimed it was the case.
After reviewing the insurance policy, the mortgage, and
other relevant documents, the insurance expert
testified...

> "It would not be uncommon for an insured who
> received a loss payment check jointly payable to
> the mortgagee, to assume that the check would
> not require the joint endorsement by the
> mortgagee under circumstances where the
> related mortgage was not attached, (or no longer
> attached) to the property that was subject to the
> claim and loss payment."

Essentially, the expert stated that not only was
the deposit of the check legal, it was also typical. As you
can see, these two expert testimonies would have been
immensely helpful for the trial and the jury. By not
obtaining these types of experts, my trial attorney really
dropped the ball. While I was fighting for freedom inside
prison, many people were fighting for me outside.

Ministry members coordinated a march in Macon and had a rally for me outside the U.S. Attorney General office in D.C. My supporters were demanding that he investigate my wrongful imprisonment.

Prominent leaders, attorney, and activist, wrote letters and advocated on my behalf, requesting my case to be opened and investigated, regarding my wrongful imprisonment and the criminal practices of the local banks.

Although many were advocating for me, the judicial system was working against me. My attorney for the appeal wrote a demand, stating that the judge should recuse himself from the case because he had previous knowledge of the case while he was a clerk. Also, he needed to remove himself from the case because, obviously, it was improbable that he would rule against and overturn the sentence of his previous mentor. He would not be able to be fair and impartial in my case. The judge refused to remove himself from the case.

After years of waiting in prison on the results of the appeal, the judge had finally made his decision. On the day of the appeal results, the ministry held a prayer vigil in the courthouse. Even with the solid arguments and expert testimonies, my appeal was denied. I would have to do my entire sentence in prison. Although many pledged their support, I struggled with the darkness of prison and with the aftermath of this conviction. However, even in the darkest place, the Lord's light shines; and even in the darkest hour, the God that I talk about is faithful to bring me through.

Chapter 11

I Still See the Good in You

Then the King will say to those at his right, "Come, you that are blessed by my Father, inherit the kingdom prepared for you from the foundation of the world; for I was hungry and you gave me food... I was in prison and you visited me. The righteous will answer, "Lord when was it that we saw you hungry... When was it that we saw you sick or in prison and visited you? And the king will answer them, "Truly I tell you, just as you did it to one of the least of these who are members of my family, you did it to me. Then he will say to those at his left, "You that are accursed, depart from me into eternal fire prepared for the devil and his followers; for I was hungry and you gave me no food, I was sick and in prison and you did not visit me.

Matthew 25:34-43 (NKJV)

Jesus reminds us that we will be judged by how we treat the outcast and marginalized of society. Often Incarcerated men and women are written off as degenerates and forgotten. They are given limited opportunities for a second chance and are labeled for the rest of their lives as felons. But there is much good in many of these men and women in prison today. I have experienced it, and I still see it. This chapter is dedicated to the stories and experiences of inmates still in the system that are doing what they can to turn their lives around. Let us always see the good in them and never forget them.

We, the People, recognize that we have responsibilities as well as rights; that our destinies are bound together; that a freedom which only asks what's in it for me, a freedom without a commitment to others, a freedom without love or charity or duty or patriotism, is unworthy of our founding ideals, and those who died in their defense.

-Barack Obama

Our Federal Criminal Justice system is in pressing need of reform. In many areas, there are millions of men and women incarcerated throughout the United States. The United States has more people incarcerated than any other developed country in the world. Often individuals are incarcerated for lengthy prison terms when probation or house arrest would have been sufficient. Prison overcrowding in the United States is commonplace.

We need a better approach to crime than mass incarceration, and we need more effective strategies to reduce recidivism. Often, after an individual has served 10-30 years in prison, they are not given resources to reintegrate into society and end up back in prison.

I commend former President Barack Obama for his efforts and support of prison reform. In recent years legislation has allowed many individuals to return home to their families and live productive lives. But it is not enough.

Further legislation is needed to eliminate mandatory minimums, increase good behavior time, and improve post-incarceration services. These changes would reduce the cost spent by the over-budget prison system and provide an incentive to people that take steps to reduce their risk of re-offending.

There are so many men and women behind bars for bad decisions and mistakes they have made. I have been taught to forgive others of their sins. Not everyone deserves an extreme punishment, many deserve a second chance. Just because someone has committed a crime, does not mean they have not learned from their mistake. Everyone has made a mistake. We were all born sinners, but through Christ, we can choose to live a righteous life, no matter our past.

I have met in prison many convicted felons that have taken the time to better themselves and turn their life around. I know of those that have left prison and achieved success, never to offend again. Those individuals have put in the dedication, determination, and patience to help themselves reintegrate into society and become a productive citizen. These people have volunteered for job training, various programs, and drug rehabilitation. I praise all the people that have taken steps to turn their life around. Yes, we are labeled "felons," but there is still good within us.

Chapter 12

Redemption

Pharaoh said to his servants, "Can we find any else like
Joseph-one in whom is the spirit of God?" So Pharaoh
said to Joseph, "Since God has shown you all this, there
is no one so discerning and wise as you. You shall be
over my house, and all my people shall order themselves
as you command... See I have set you over all the land of
Egypt." Removing his signet ring from his hand,
Pharaoh put it on Joseph's hand, he arrayed him in
garments of fine linen, and put a gold chain around his
neck. He had him ride in the chariot of his
second-in-command; and they cried out in front
of him, "Bow the Knee!"

Genesis 41:38-43 (ESV)

In the years of his youth, Joseph dreamt of Greatness. He
dreamt that he would rise up and others would bow
before him. Yet, Joseph went from a favored son to a
slave, from a slave to a prisoner. From the outside, it
looked like Joseph was going down, not up. Surely, no
one in Egypt was going to kneel before a Hebrew slave
in prison. But God never abandoned Joseph, and Joseph
remained faithful, eventually seeing God's promise
delivered. It is important to remember that although we
may not always understand His ways, God uses us for
His greater purpose. Had Joseph not been sold to an
Egyptian, had he not gone to prison, the Nation of Israel,

God's chosen people, would have starved in famine. Joseph was charged with the care of a nation, whatever he asked for, it was done. He made it through the fire to find redemption. So too, do I faithfully anticipate redemption in my story. I know God is not done with me yet and will use me to do great things for his purpose.

Now there is a final reason I think that Jesus says, "Love your enemies." It is this: that love has within it a redemptive power. And there is a power there that eventually transforms individuals. Just keep being friendly to that person. Just keep loving them, and they can't stand it too long. Oh, they react in many ways in the beginning. They react with guilt feelings, and sometimes they'll hate you a little more at that transition period, but just keep loving them. And by the power of your love, they will break down under the load. That's love, you see. It is redemptive, and this is why Jesus says love. There's something about love that builds up and is creative. There is something about hate that tears down and is destructive. So, love your enemies.

-Martin Luther King Jr.

For the eight years that I worked for the ministry, never did I receive a salary. I made millions of dollars while traveling by selling my products. I had built an excellent reputation with my bank, and every year, they would donate property to the foundation I started. While incarcerated, I continued to support my family and children with money that I had saved through personal investments. At my sentencing hearing, the Judge himself brought up the fact that I had donated 10,000 jackets to individuals in need in Flint, Michigan. The jackets that I gave away were worth more than the money I was accused of stealing. With the blessings God had placed over my life, I never had any reason to take or engage in any fraudulent acts.

In 1st Peter 5:10 it says, "And the God of grace, who called you to his eternal glory in Christ, after you have suffered a little while, will himself restore you and make you strong, firm, and steadfast. To him be the power forever and ever, Amen." I believe that this is the case for me. My suffering has made me strong in Christ.

I was publicly humiliated, had my reputation destroyed, and thrown in prison for 10 years for a crime I never committed. I lost material things and friends. I lost people that I thought would stand by me through thick and thin.

Before I came to prison, people would come to me, ask me for money and things. I gave openly, but many of these same people disappeared when I got arrested. Someone prophesied before my sentence and said that "I had been good to everybody, so for those that want to walk away, do it now." I suppose he foresaw that many would walk out on me. Forces tried to destroy me, but what was intended for evil, God has used for good.

This experience has brought out the best in me. I dedicated my time to keep my spirits up by studying, learning, reading, praying, and listening to the gospel.

There is no timing like God's timing. I told myself that God had a plan for me that was bigger than myself. I had to become a wounded healer. Battling the devil himself was a part of my destiny. I have overcome so much, and today I stand, a stronger brethren, knowing that within the power of prayer, everything is possible. I have found through the suffering, a deeper purpose for my life. I believe that our Lord and Savior had to bring me down to build me back up, like a potter perfecting clay. I had to lose it all so I could give my testimony and save others.

I am forever thankful to every person that stood by me through the journey. Their acts of kindness, whether it was a card, a letter, a visit, or accepting my call, kept me strong and had a significant impact on keeping my spirits alive. The greatest moment for me while I have been incarcerated was receiving the news that the new ministry was finally completed. It was built debt-free with no institutional funding. I was so excited that I cried tears of joy.

Today, I stand ready to exit this place and to be restored and installed as a leader of my ministry. God has given me the ability to return and finish what my father, grandfather, and I started years ago. I plan to use my experience to help those that are still incarcerated and often forgotten. I will be their advocate. I will go before politicians to advocate for prison reform.

This book will be a tool to educate the public about what can happen in our judicial system. I plan to do a talk show called "Power for Life," in which men and women that are incarcerated across the country will be able to write and tell their stories. This show will be about them and their struggle. I will do everything I can to provide additional re-entry and educational opportunities to those leaving prison. One of these projects is the Rosa Maw School of Culinary Arts.

I will advocate among business owners, and if you are a business owner or manager reading this, hear me today. If someone does not show these people returning from prison, the grace of Christ, if someone does not offer these people a second chance, they will likely be lost to the system once more. I am ready, for God has ignited a fire in me and will use me as his vessel. I am walking in my divine destiny.

Appendix

A – I assume would be a copy of the mortgage
B - I assume would be a copy of the quick claim deed

FACT SHEET REGARDING PASTOR ONSLOW ROSS

I. The Loan Payback by The Church And Security Bank's Arguably Illegal Conduct

Essentially, Security Bank- the same bank whose representative (Charles Blankenship) sent a letter to the DA accusing Pastor Ross of forgery/fraud and asking that he be brought to justice- has **possibly** committed insurance fraud. At the very least, an investigation could be called for, even though the bank has closed.

The Church repaid the $520,000.00 loan. What seems to be meant by that is the initial $520,000.00 was paid in full because at the time CB&T received a wire transfer of $476,622.29 (in December 2006), CB&T took $87,622.29 to pay off the Church's remaining debt from the $117,000.00 demand letter made by CB&T, to the Church, in February 2006.

a. Facts

Ms. Gomez, stipulated in court that money from a wire transfer to CB&T ($476,622.29) was allegedly released to Security Bank to pay back the subject $389,000.00 (**Ex. 1**, for copy of Court Transcript regarding stipulation). The wire transfer was for $476,622.29 (**Ex. 2**). According to the trial transcript CB&T sent Security Bank $389,000.00 (**Ex. 3**) of that money. $476,622.29- $389,000.00= $87,622.29. According to payment records of the Church's payments to CB&T on the $520,000.00 mortgage, CB&T received a payment on 12/14/2006 of exactly $87, 622.29. (**Ex. 5**.) The Church paid off the loan.

So CB&T got the wire transfer, paid themselves the remaining balance on the Church's loan, and then supposedly sent the $389,000.00 to Security Bank.

b. The Problem

ASSUMING CB&T Bank actually sent the $389,000.00 to Security Bank, Charles Blankenship, Security Officer and Fraud Investigator for Security Bank, states in the trial transcript that Security Bank's private insurance paid Security Bank $289,000.00 of the $389,000.00 loss (amount paid to CB&T in January 2006). (See **Ex. 6**.) That means that unless Security Bank paid back the insurance company the $289,000.00 of the $389,000.00 it received from CB&T in January 2006 - Security Bank never returned any of the $289,000.00 of insurance reimbursement to the insurance company, even though Security bank allegedly regained the entire $389,000.00 it paid out to CB&T because CB&T allegedly returned the full $389,000.00 to Security Bank. **That's potential fraud that needs to be investigated.**

If true, how can a bank accuse a person of forgery and fraud knowing it committed fraud itself, mindful that **ALL THE ABOVE OCCURRED AFTER PASTOR ROSS' INDICTMENT BUT BEFORE HIS TRIAL.**

II. Representation

Debra Gomes has admitted that she did not consult insurance experts regarding the original trial of the case. (Ex.7 ¶ 7) That's significant because since Onslow Ross has been incarcerated, two experts have said the following:

1. The insurance expert supports the assertion that the check could have been issued without naming CB& T Bank and that it is not unusual for a an insured such as the Church to attempt to cash the check without the endorsement of the Bank since the Bank did not have a perfected title (Ex. 8, p. 6); and

2. The Mortgage Expert states that CB&T did not have title to the property at issue. (EX. 9 ¶ 14.)

III. Other Bank Issues

Essentially it appears that some type of fraud is going on-

a. CB&T

On February 2, 2006 CB&T Bank made a demand for $117,717.07 to the Church. (Ex. 10.) because CB&T received the $389,000 insurance proceeds from Security bank after demanding those proceeds in early December 2005. (See Ex. 3, trial transcript.)

- Problem

Stephen Williams then vice-president of CB&T Bank admits that in November 2005 (BEFORE the demand to Security Bank for the $389,000), their attorney Robert Tuggle told him that "your lien does not look perfected." (Ex. 11.) LOOK at the Mortgage Expert Report (Ex. 9) which confirms that the lean was not perfected. So that means an argument can be made that CB&T made the demand in bad faith and maliciously. YOU NEED TO GET THE LETTER REFERRED TO IN EXHIBIT 11.

- You'd think if a VP was told that by an attorney, then, he would have had an expert take a look also (I bet he did). Was any discovery done on this issue?

b. Security Bank

So Security bank pays out the $389,000, THEN, on February 1, 2006 Charles Blankenship of Security Bank sends a letter to the District Attorney's Office, stating "Security Bank of Bibb County is the victim of the $389,000 checked forged by Onslow Ross...." (Ex.12.) The problem with this letter, amongst other things:

1. *Expert testimony establishes that to a high probability Onslow Ross did not sign the check, so the forgery statement made by Security Bank is most likely false* (Ex. 13, for expert handwriting report); and

2. The teller that received the check refused to submit to a handwriting sample and that Attorney Gomez did not move to compel him to submit to a handwriting sample. (Ex. 7 ¶ 10.) The issue is

although Security Bank's letter accuses Ross of forgery, you'd think they would have done a handwriting sample before making such a statement. I think they did and no one pressed that issue—this is inconsequential but if this goes further, you should see if you could talk to this person.

Call me, so we can discuss further.

1   (Jurors enter courtroom)

2   THE COURT: Good morning, ladies and gentlemen. I

3   appreciate you being prompt this morning. I will let you know

4   that when I ask you to be back at 9:00, that's when I plan to

5   start the trial of the case each day, but it's not uncommon at

6   all for me to have to deal with certain legal issues with the

7   attorneys. And typically, if I am dealing with those issues

8   outside of your hearing, that is, when you are back in the jury

9   room, I can move forward with them much faster than if you were

10   here. If you're here, I have to do it over here, and that makes

11   it complicated. But I will tell you also that yesterday after

12   you left at 5:00, we stayed for a while after that, and talked

13   about a number of issues in the case, and tried to streamline

14   the case.

15   It is a very important responsibility of the trial

16   judge to make sure that the case moves along, and that the

17   evidence that comes in is really focused on the issues in the

18   case, and as a consequence, the parties reached a stipulation

19   yesterday. A stipulation is something that the parties agree

20   to. It is something that does not have to be proven, and it's

21   something that you should accept as proven. And I'm going to

22   read this stipulation to you. "The parties in this case have

23   stipulated that Reaching Souls Cathedral of Praise obtained a

24   loan from Foundation Capital Resources through a broker called

25   Unlimited Funding, which was then paid to CB&T Bank, in

126

1 settlement of a civil lawsuit for repayment of the funds

2 received from Alfa Insurance Company. CB&T Bank, in turn,

3 released those funds to Security Bank." I caution you that

4 repayment is neither a defense to the charge of bank fraud, nor

5 material to the crime. You may consider this subsequent payment

6 only to the extent that it is material to the Defendant's

7 defense of good faith, and only to the extent that it may be

8 evidence of Defendant's good faith at the time Defendant

9 presented the check from Alfa Insurance for deposit at Security

10 Bank on August 23rd, 2005. All right. Did you finish with the

11 witness?

12   MR. CHRISTIAN: Yes, Your Honor. He's on cross.

13   CROSS EXAMINATION

14 BY MS. GOMEZ:

15 Q   Good morning, Mr. Williams.

16 A   Good morning.

17 Q   Mr. Williams, when you testified yesterday about your visit

18 from Pastor Ross and Lucille Davis, is it not true, sir, that

19 when they came to see you it was shortly after the collapse of

20 the church, correct?

21 A   No, it wasn't.

22 Q   It wasn't?

23 A   It was in June.

24 Q   June when?

25 A   I don't know the date. I just know that when I set my

TAMMY W. FLETCHER - US COURT REPORTER - 478-752-3497

Wire Transfer Order
First American Title Company, LLC

Number: 5445

File No :	NCS-259669-HOUt	Issued By:	Read T. Hammond
PR:	NATLAC - National Commercial Services Division	Issued Date/Time:	12/12/2006 12:36:22 PM
Office:	15 - Houston-NCSD (1550)	Transmission Date/Time:	12/12/2006
Officer:	PJ Whitworth	Amount:	$476,622.29

ORIGINATOR

Account Number	Bank Name
08806367205	JPMorgan Chase Bank -

Information
259669

RECEIVING BANK

ABA Number	Bank Name
061100606	Columbia Bank & Trust for further credit to CB&T Bank of Middle

Bank Address

BENEFICIARY

Account Number	Beneficiary Name
0027205483	CB&T Bank

Beneficiary Address
P.O. box 2107; Warner Robins, GA 31099

Additional Information
Payoff Loan No. 27205483/10 - Read

CUSTOMER AUTHORIZATION

Signature	Signature
Printed Name and Title	Printed Name and Title

BANK USE ONLY

Fund Held/Credit	Credit Code	CALLBACK	
Available Funds		Name	
		Time	Initials
Fees		Method of Payment	
☐ Analysis ☐ Charge To Account		☐ Debit Account Number	☐ Check Received
☐ Waived ☐ Included in Check			
☐ Other		☐ Incoming Wire	☐ Other

SPECIAL INSTRUCTIONS/NOTES

PLAINTIFF'S
EXHIBIT
3

26

1   please?

2   THE COURT: Certainly.

3   MR. CHRISTIAN: We have no objection, Your Honor.

4   THE COURT: It's admitted.

5   MS. GOMEZ: Mr. Christian, there's another portion

6   that I'm going to introduce; that's the pack that I gave you

7   last week.

8   BY MS. GOMEZ:

9   Q   I'm going to have you turn specifically to page two.

10   MS. GOMEZ: Your Honor, may I publish this, please,

11   I'm going to use the Government's?

12   THE COURT: Yes.

13   BY MS. GOMEZ:

14   Q   Mr. Williams, while that's heating up a little bit, let me

15   go ahead and ask you this.

16   A   Okay.

17   Q   At some point you made a demand upon Security Bank for

18   389,000; is that correct?

19   A   That's correct.

20   Q   Do you remember when you made that demand?

21   A   It had to be December of '05, once I found out the check

22   had been -- we had received a copy of it. And we filed the

23   affidavit with Regions, which is what we are supposed to do, and

24   then contacted Security that we had filed this affidavit.

25   Q   Were those proceeds turned over to you after your demand

27

1   was made?

2   A   Security Bank paid us the amount of the check, yes.

3   Q   And that amount was applied to the outstanding debt?

4   A   Yes, it was.

5   Q   Now, you have already told us that this letter, this

6   commitment letter --

7   MS. GOMEZ: Mr. Green, could you please enlarge the

8   part where the appraisal is?

9   BY MS. GOMEZ:

10 Q   You already said that this was a loan commitment letter

11 done in November of 2003?

12 A   Yes.

13 Q   Sir, and here in your second page of that loan commitment

14 letter you say that the appraisal of the property must be for at

15 least $715,000?

16 A   Yes.

17 Q   Yet after being given the insurance proceeds of 389,000, at

18 some point, you said shortly, in December, after you made your

19 demand?

20 A   Yes.

21 Q   Is it not true, sir, that you still then proceeded to have

22 your attorney, Mr. Tuggle, again try to foreclose on the church

23 to get the balance on the note; is that correct?

24 A   Absolutely.

25 Q   Okay.

36

1   made on the note to CB&T Bank?

2   A   Yes, they're starting to make their payments.

3   MS. GOMEZ: Mr. Green, next screen, please.

4   BY MS. GOMEZ:

5   Q   At what point was the $389,000 applied to the note?

6   A   It says here on February the 2nd.

7   Q   And that is the amount that you received from Security

8   Bank, correct?

9   A   Yes.

10   Q   And at that point we have the loan balance reduced to

11   $110,586.56?

12   A   Yes.

13   Q   And that is the point that you then decided to go ahead and

14   foreclose on the rest of the note through your attorney, Mr.

15   Tuggle?

16   A   Yes.

17   MS. GOMEZ: Next screen, please.

18   BY MS. GOMEZ:

19   Q   Mr. Williams, would you agree that in February 28th of '06,

20   and then in March 31st of '06 once again you see continued

21   mortgage payments being made by the church?

22   A   Yes.   They were late, but they were making them.

23   Q   Being made, once again, on that balance, the now balance of

24   $110,000 is being reduced every month?

25   A   Yes.

Page: 1 Document Name: untitled

LNHSS   HISTORY SUMMARY SCREEN   02/13/08 12:16:59
                    272   CB&T BANK

PROC DATE 02/13/08 REACHING SOULS CATHEDRAL PAGE REQUEST: 001 PAGE NO: 001
ACCOUNT: 00027205483 NOTE: 00010   PART: SEQ:
DATE RANGE: ALL   POST/EFF DATE: INCLUDE FEE HIST(Y/N): Y
SORT OPTION (P/E): E   ASCEND/DESCEND: D   TRANS RANGE: 000 999

ACT EFF DATE	POST DATE	TC R	TRANS AMOUNT	LOAN BALANCE	DESCRIPTION
12/12/06	12/14/06	650	87,622.29	0.00	PAYOFF
12/12/06	12/14/06	650	200.00		PAYOFF
12/12/06	12/14/06	650	60.00		PAYOFF
12/12/06	12/14/06	650	432.00		PAYOFF
11/15/06	11/15/06	761	100.00		LATE FEE ASSESS
11/09/06	11/09/06	680	135.00		FEE PAYMENT
11/09/06	11/09/06	760	135.00		MAN FEE ASSESS
10/16/06	10/16/06	761	100.00		LATE FEE ASSESS
10/03/06	10/03/06	610	4,167.17	85,471.06	REGULAR PAYMENT
10/03/06	10/03/06	610	100.00		REGULAR PAYMENT
09/15/06	09/15/06	761	100.00		LATE FEE ASSESS
09/14/06	09/14/06	610	4,314.00	88,968.06	REGULAR PAYMENT
09/14/06	09/14/06	610	46.83		REGULAR PAYMENT

PRESS PA1 FOR NEXT PAGE

Page: 1 Document Name: untitled

<pre>
LNHSS   HISTORY SUMMARY SCREEN   02/13/08 12:16:59
                        272   CB&T BANK

PROC DATE 02/13/08 REACHING SOULS CATHEDRAL PAGE REQUEST: 001 PAGE NO: 002
ACCOUNT: 00027205483 NOTE: 00010   PART: SEQ:
DATE RANGE: ALL   POST/EFF DATE: INCLUDE FEE HIST(Y/N): Y
SORT OPTION (P/E): E   ASCEND/DESCEND: D   TRANS RANGE: 000 999

ACT EFF DATE POST DATE TC R   TRANS AMOUNT LOAN BALANCE   DESCRIPTION
   09/13/06 09/13/06 610   4,220.34   92,436.20 REGULAR PAYMENT
   09/13/06 09/13/06 610   153.17   REGULAR PAYMENT
   08/15/06 08/15/06 761   100.00   LATE FEE ASSESS
   07/24/06 07/24/06 610   4,167.17   95,926.35 REGULAR PAYMENT
   07/24/06 07/24/06 610   100.00   REGULAR PAYMENT
   07/17/06 07/17/06 761   100.00   LATE FEE ASSESS
   06/15/06 06/15/06 761   100.00   LATE FEE ASSESS
   06/09/06 06/09/06 760   60.00   MAN FEE ASSESS
   06/01/06 06/01/06 610   4,167.17   99,377.81 REGULAR PAYMENT
   06/01/06 06/01/06 610   100.00   REGULAR PAYMENT
   05/19/06 05/19/06 760   432.00   MAN FEE ASSESS
   05/17/06 05/17/06 810   162.00-   FEE REVERSAL
   05/17/06 05/17/06 760*   162.00   MAN FEE ASSESS

PRESS PA1 FOR NEXT PAGE, PF13 FOR PREVIOUS PAGE
</pre>

Page: 1 Document Name: untitled

LNHSS   HISTORY SUMMARY SCREEN   02/13/08 12:16:59
                          272   CB&T BANK

PROC DATE 02/13/08 REACHING SOULS CATHEDRAL PAGE REQUEST: 001 PAGE NO: 003
ACCOUNT: 00027205483 NOTE: 00010   PART: SEQ:
DATE RANGE: ALL   POST/EFF DATE: INCLUDE FEE HIST(Y/N): Y
SORT OPTION (P/E): E   ASCEND/DESCEND: D   TRANS RANGE: 000 999

ACT EFF DATE	POST DATE	TC R	TRANS AMOUNT	LOAN BALANCE	DESCRIPTION
05/15/06	05/15/06	761	100.00		LATE FEE ASSESS
04/26/06	04/26/06	610	4,167.17	102,833.05	REGULAR PAYMENT
04/26/06	04/26/06	610	100.00		REGULAR PAYMENT
04/21/06	04/25/06	800	670.03-	106,240.66	REVERSAL
04/21/06	04/21/06	725	670.03	106,240.66	LOAN FEES
04/21/06	04/21/06	725*	670.03	105,570.63	NOTE INCREASE ADJ
04/21/06	04/21/06	680	670.03		FEE PAYMENT
04/21/06	04/21/06	760	670.03		MAN FEE ASSESS
04/17/06	04/17/06	761	100.00		LATE FEE ASSESS
03/31/06	03/31/06	610	4,167.17	105,570.63	REGULAR PAYMENT
03/31/06	03/31/06	610	100.00		REGULAR PAYMENT
03/15/06	03/15/06	761	100.00		LATE FEE ASSESS
02/28/06	03/02/06	610	4,167.17	109,582.73	NONPOST

PRESS PA1 FOR NEXT PAGE, PF13 FOR PREVIOUS PAGE

Date: 2/13/2008 Time: 1:17:15 PM

Page: 1 Document Name: untitled

LNHSS   HISTORY SUMMARY SCREEN   02/13/08 12:16:59
                      272   CB&T BANK

PROC DATE 02/13/08 REACHING SOULS CATHEDRAL PAGE REQUEST: 001 PAGE NO: 004
ACCOUNT: 00027205483 NOTE: 00010   PART: SEQ:
DATE RANGE: ALL   POST/EFF DATE: INCLUDE FEE HIST(Y/N): Y
SORT OPTION (P/E): E   ASCEND/DESCEND: D   TRANS RANGE: 000 999

ACT EFF DATE POST DATE TC R   TRANS AMOUNT   LOAN BALANCE   DESCRIPTION
   02/28/06   03/02/06   610   100.00   REGULAR PAYMENT
   02/15/06   02/15/06   761   100.00   LATE FEE ASSESS
   02/02/06   02/03/06   660   389,000.00   110,586.56   SPECIAL PAYMENT
   01/31/06   01/31/06   610   4,997.34   499,586.56   REGULAR PAYMENT
   01/31/06   01/31/06   610   930.17   REGULAR PAYMENT
   01/24/06   01/31/06   800   380,865.66-   500,598.76   ENDORSEMENT MISSI
   01/24/06   01/31/06   800   8,134.34-   500,598.76   REVERSAL
   01/24/06   01/25/06   668*   380,865.66   500,598.76   SYST GEN PYMT
   01/24/06   01/25/06   610*   8,134.34   500,598.76   REGULAR PAYMENT
   01/17/06   01/17/06   761   100.00   LATE FEE ASSESS
   01/12/06   01/12/06   680   108.00   FEE PAYMENT
   01/12/06   01/12/06   760   108.00   MAN FEE ASSESS
   01/09/06   01/12/06   725   108.00   500,598.76   LOAN FEES

PRESS PA1 FOR NEXT PAGE, PF13 FOR PREVIOUS PAGE

Date: 2/13/2008 Time: 1:17:22 PM

Page: 1 Document Name: untitled

LNHSS   HISTORY SUMMARY SCREEN   02/13/08 12:16:59
                         272   CB&T BANK

PROC DATE 02/13/08 REACHING SOULS CATHEDRAL PAGE REQUEST: 001 PAGE NO: 005
ACCOUNT: 00027205463 NOTE: 00010   PART: SEQ:
DATE RANGE: ALL   POST/EFF DATE: INCLUDE FEE HIST(Y/N): Y
SORT OPTION (P/E): E   ASCEND/DESCEND: D TRANS RANGE: 000 999

ACT EFF DATE	POST DATE	TC R	TRANS AMOUNT	LOAN BALANCE	DESCRIPTION
01/09/06	01/12/06	810	108.00-		FEE REVERSAL
01/09/06	01/12/06	810	108.00-		FEE REVERSAL
01/09/06	01/09/06	680*	108.00		FEE PAYMENT
01/09/06	01/09/06	760*	108.00		MAN FEE ASSESS
12/07/05	12/07/05	610	4,067.17	500,490.76	REGULAR PAYMENT
11/09/05	11/09/05	610	4,067.17	501,594.71	REGULAR PAYMENT
10/11/05	10/11/05	610	4,067.17	502,594.53	REGULAR PAYMENT
09/29/05	09/30/05	613	4,067.17	503,662.56	REGULAR PAYMENT
09/15/05	09/15/05	761	100.00		LATE FEE ASSESS
09/02/05	09/02/05	610	8,134.34	504,659.44	REGULAR PAYMENT
08/15/05	08/15/05	761	100.00		LATE FEE ASSESS
07/28/05	07/28/05	610	4,067.17	506,680.25	REGULAR PAYMENT
07/15/05	07/15/05	761	100.00		LATE FEE ASSESS

PRESS PA1 FOR NEXT PAGE, PF13 FOR PREVIOUS PAGE

1 can make suggestions as to what size, but we could be overruled

2 by the regulators.

3 Q   So whenever the bank suffers a loss you attempt to reduce

4 the loss?

5 A   We attempted to reduce this loss. In this case we had a

6 $100,000 deductible. We filed a claim to the insurance company,

7 in which case we were reimbursed the amount of $289,000; and, of

8 course, we paid the $100,000 deductible.

9 Q   Thank you. Government's Exhibit 57, tell us what that is,

10 please?

11 A   Exhibit 57 is a Security Bank certified check dated 9-9-05

12 in the amount of $49,000 payable to Willie Ross with the

13 remitter of Willie Ross.

14   MR. CHRISTIAN: We would tender that check at this

15 time, please, Your Honor.

16   MS. GOMEZ: No objection, Your Honor.

17   THE COURT: Admitted.

18 BY MR. CHRISTIAN:

19 Q   I'm going to show you Government's Exhibits 58, 59, and 60,

20 and tell us if you recognize those?

21 A   Yes, sir. Government's Exhibit 58 is our teller accepting

22 a deposit. The next frame is Government's Exhibit 59 with a

23 picture of Onslow Ross walking up, it appears at this point, to

24 a CSR desk. Government's Exhibit 60 is Onslow Ross standing at

25 the teller line making a transaction, and this is dated 9-19-05.

1   asking Ms. Klein for assistance in the prosecution of Mr. Ross?

2   A   Uh-huh. (Affirmative).

3   Q   My question for you is, approximately December 20th of '05,

4   is that when you became aware of the alleged fraud, or did you

5   become aware of that sooner, concerning this check?

6   A   I was aware of it sooner, but to give you an exact date I

7   cannot recall. I wrote this letter on this particular date from

8   notes I had made previously.

9   Q   You answered earlier that the failure of Security Bank

10   could clearly affect your ability to have this FDIC insurance

11   that's required to run a bank. The $389,000 loss to Security

12   Bank, would you admit that's a pretty substantial loss for a

13   bank your size?

14   A   Yes, ma'am, but let me clarify something. The insurance is

15   private insurance. The bond has nothing to do with the FDIC.

16   We purchase that. That's private insurance. The matter I was

17   referring to that would affect the bank is the licensing of our

18   bank and the governing of our bank. It has nothing to do with

19   the insurance.

20   Q   So let me get this right. The insurance, the private

21   insurance paid the 389,000 or the 100,000?

22   A   The private insurance paid 289,000. We ourself insured up

23   to $100,000.

24   Q   But your licensing could be affected by the violation of

25   the procedures for the deposit of the check?

Case 5:07-cr-00077-CAR-CWH   Document 99-5   Filed 07/08/2010   Page 1 of 2

Affidavit supporting Onslow Ross's 2255
Middle District of Georgia (Macon Division) 5:07-CR-00077-CAR

I, Debra G. Gómez, hereby affirm to the following:

1. I am an attorney licensed to practice law in the state of Georgia.

2. I represented Onslow Ross at trial in case number 5:07-CR-00077-CAR.

3. I am aware Onslow Ross is filing a 2255, Habeas Corpus petition.

4. I have reviewed the petition and state the following:

5. In regards to Issue III of Petitioner's 2255 petition, I did not consult with any experts in the insurance or mortgage fields.

6. I presented the testimony of Robin Taviner, a professional title searcher, that there was no mortgage on the damaged property alleged to be the object of insurance fraud, but I did not consult with a mortgage expert on the effect of Mr. Taviner's testimony or the proper conclusions to be drawn from his testimony.

7. I did not consult with an insurance expert to determine how or why the bank's name appeared on the insurance check or what a layperson would have thought having received such a check, knowing that there was no mortgage with that bank on the damaged property.

8. I did not discuss with Mr. Ross or his family the possibility of consulting with a mortgage or insurance expert or their usefulness in presenting the case to the jury.

9. I did not refrain from consulting with or presenting expert testimony for any strategic reason.

10. In regards to Issue V of Petitioner's 2255 petition, I did not file a motion to compel Mr. Josh Jones to submit to a handwriting exemplar.

11. I was aware that Mr. Ross's handwriting was not a match for the signature on the insurance check, and that Mr. Jones was terminated from his position at Security Bank in wrongfully cashing that check.

12. I was aware that I could file a motion to compel Mr. Jones to submit to a handwriting sample, however, I did not do so.

13. Mr. Ross informed me that he was afraid of testifying.

139

14. Mr. Ross had a criminal record, which is usually a significant reason for a defendant not to testify in a case.

15. I was aware of various other forms of impeaching information, including a loan application in which Mr. Ross's income was overstated.

16. I did not fully inform Mr. Ross that these items could be used to impeach his credibility in the event that he testified.

17. I advised Mr. Ross of my recommendation that he need to testify in order to explain an allegation that he impersonated his grandmother over the phone. However, I did not fully explain that even when he testified to a limited scope of material, he could be impeached by any and all of the above listed information and that cross-examination would not necessarily be limited by the scope of his direct testimony.

I affirm that the above is true and correct to the best of my knowledge and belief.

04/27/2010
Date

Debra G. Gómez, Esq.
1469 Oglethorpe Street
Macon, GA 31208

Notary

Sworn to and subscribed before me
This 27th day of April 2010.

A Notary Public
Of the State of Georgia, Bibb County
My Commission expires: 02/04/2015

140

In The Matter of
Reaching Souls Cathedral of Praise
And Certain Individuals Thereto

On Appeal to the
United States Court of Appeal

Expert Report
Submitted by
William D. Hager
To and For Marcia G. Shein,
Attorney at Law
Federal Criminal Law Center
In this Matter on Appeal

141

TABLE OF CONTENTS

APPENDICES

I. INTRODUCTION

Introduction. I have been retained as an insurance expert consultant (expert witness) by the law firm of Marcia G. Shein, P.C., of the Federal Criminal Law Center (sometimes, "Shein") on behalf of certain individuals of the Reaching Souls Cathedral of Praise ("Cathedral of Praise") as to the appeal of the criminal conviction of certain individual(s) affiliated with the Cathedral of Praise. These opinions will be used by Shein in fashioning her appeal as to affected individuals.

Qualification to Render These Expert Opinions. Each of the expert opinions and conclusions in this report are based on my skill, knowledge, training, education, expertise and experience, that are set out in detail (i) in my attached Curriculum Vitae (see Appendix A) and (ii) below under Section V of this Report, setting out specific expertise.

Prevailing Industry Standards. Each of the expert opinions in this report, in addition to other support set forth in the opinions, is based on prevailing standards in the insurance industry, including custom and practice, except as qualified. As such, the opinions are based on what a reasonably prudent insurer would and should do in comparable circumstances.

Documents Reviewed in Reaching All of These Expert Opinions and Conclusions. In reaching each of the expert opinions and conclusions in this report, I utilized the all of the documents and data referenced in this report.

Foundation to All of the Opinions. Thus, each of the expert opinions and conclusions in this report are based in a combination of (i) this author's skill, knowledge, training, education, expertise, experience and working knowledge of the specific areas and matters at issue herein, (ii) prevailing standards in the industry and (iii) documents cited. Of course, all of the opinions in this report are limited to the unique facts of this case. I have reached these opinions based on a reasonable degree of professional certainty.

Additional Documents. I am submitting this report on the specific matters set out below in connection with this litigation. I understand that additional documents may be forthcoming and as such, I reserve the right to amend and otherwise modify this report including its summaries, opinions and all other elements and additional comments by opposing experts.

Limitations of All of These Expert Opinions. These entire expert opinions and conclusions relate to and are specifically limited to the unique facts of this case; as such, these opinions do not have applicability beyond the facts of this case.

Compensation. I am being compensated at the rate of $495 per hour for my work on this case, with a minimum charge of $5,000. This is my usual and customary rate.

III. DOCUMENTS REVIEWED

Sources of Information. I obtained documents and used resources from: (i) the Law Office of Marcia G. Shein, P.C., as more fully detailed below, (ii) industry sources including my own insurance library, (iii) standard property casualty insurance reference materials, (iv) certain regulatory, statutory and case law materials including that of Georgia and (v) certain regulatory materials from the National Association of Insurance Commissioners ("NAIC") as those materials relate to and are utilized by the Georgia Department of Insurance (sometimes, the "GDOI") .

In that regard and in connection with preparing this opinion, I was provided and I reviewed among others, the following documents inclusive of attachments and exhibits as applicable:

1. The insurance application and supplemental application related to this matter;

2. Alfa Insurance Corporation's ("Alpha") Worksheet, which is part of the policy at issue (i.e., policy No. SM 042742);

3. Certain reinsurance information as to the policy;

4. Certain communications relating to the application at issue;

5. The Commercial Deed to Secure Debt and Security Agreement at issue;

6. Certain communications (CB & T to Cathedral of Praise) relating to the insurance proceeds and default;

7. Certain Commercial Loan Application materials;

8. Certain elements of the insurance policy at issue;

9. Certain billing notices relating to the policy;

10. Certain communication from Alfa terminating the policy at issue;

11. Certain information about the property loss at issue;

12. Complaint and Answer in the matter of CB & T of Middle Georgia (sometimes, "CB & T") vs. Reaching Souls, Onslow Ross, Lucile Davis and Undre Williams;

13. Complaint in the matter of Reaching Souls vs. CB & T;

14. Various National Association of Insurance Commissioners ("NAIC") model acts and model regulations as they relate to the GDOI;

15. NAIC's Market Conduct Examiners Handbooks (renamed: Market Regulation Handbook), Volume I as utilized by the GDOI in matters such as those at issue here;

16. Various case law and state statutory and state administrative provisions of Georgia relating to insurance;

17. Various on-line websites; and

18. Others.

III. ASSIGNMENT AND EXPERT OPINIONS AND FURTHER DISCUSSION

Assignment. My assignment was to read and review various records and documents in this case and enter expert opinions, if any, as to whether the related loss payment check ('check") issued by Alfa was required to be made payable to (among others) CB & T, given the related mortgage and policy language at issue.

SUMMARY OF EXPERT OPINIONS

Prior to setting out my expert opinions (below) on this matter, I have set out in this section, (i) certain assumptions Shein asked me to make in entering these opinions and (ii) certain factual considerations.

Assumptions. In connection with entering my opinions, I was asked by Shein to assume (and I have assumed) the following:

- That the mortgage at issue did not attach to the property upon which the loss occurred (along these lines, note my related statement below);

- That the two buildings covered by the policy had different addresses;[1]

- The sole insurance policy at issue is policy No. SM 042742;

Statement of Facts. In addition, the following facts are pivotal to my opinions:

- The policy contained the following Mortgagee Clause:

  "Loss, if any, under this policy, shall be payable to the following mortgagee(s) as their interest may appear, subject to provisions of the mortgagee clause appearing on the reverse side of this form. CB & T Bank; PO Box 11209, Jacksonville FL 32239, Loan # 27205483-10.

---

[1] The policy application shows but one address for the two buildings.

- The policy's Mortgagee Clause continued (on the following page of the policy), providing in part as follows:

  "Loss, if any, on building items under this policy, shall be payable to the mortgagee ... as provided herein, as interest may appear ... "

- The application at issue for among others, property coverage, shows two buildings (a "Worship Center") at Location #1 and a "Church" at Location #2;[2]

- I have not and did not do any analysis of the mortgage at issue and do not have and do not express any expert opinions as to the mortgage (including to what and how the mortgage may or may not have attached to the property at issue) and have no particular expertise as to mortgages. Along these lines, as to the mortgage, I have simply made those assumptions I was asked to make by Shein.

Expert Opinion Number One: Given these assumptions, although it would have required analysis by Alfa, including the kind of additional analysis not typically undertaken by insurers under facts such as those at issue here, Alfa could have issued the check without naming CB & T as a payee on the check to the extent Alfa concluded that the mortgage did not attach to the property that was the subject of the loss. Alfa was not required to do such analysis nor was Alfa required to issue the check without naming CB & T; only that Alfa could have so issued the check without naming CB & T as a payee, given the stated assumptions and facts. Included in such assumptions would have been a requirement that Alfa concluded that the key loss payee language permitted it to go behind the Mortgagee Clause and analyze the related mortgage (the key loss payee language, as stated, provided as follow: "Loss, if any, on building items under this policy, shall be payable to the mortgagee ... as provided herein, *as interest may appear ...* [3]).

Expert Opinion Number Two: Based on my experience in such matters, it would not be uncommon for an insured who received a loss payment check jointly payable to the mortgagee under circumstances where the related mortgage did not attach (or no longer attached) to the property that was the subject of the loss payment to assume that the check would not then require the joint endorsement by the mortgagee.

Expert Opinion Number Three: Given the uniqueness of the situation here, based on my experience in such matters, few if any insureds applying for coverage, would recognize and understand that it would be in their interest (and they could if they wanted to) to (i) apply for two separate policies, one covering the mortgaged property and

---

[2] See the Alfa Insurance Corporation Church Application/ Georgia carrying a (presumably received by Alfa) stamp date of 4/27/2005.

[3] Emphasis added. This is so because the phrase "... as interest may appear ... " can be read to grant Alfa the authority to determine the manner in which the mortgage's "interest may appear". Similarly Alfa could have done what they in fact did here, namely to have issued the check naming CB & T as payee on the check.

another policy covering the property without the mortgage or (ii) alternatively to file appropriate documents with the insurer at the inception of the policy making clear that the mortgage only attached to one of two portions of the property at issue, thereby eliminating, upon loss, the very situation that arose here, namely a loss payment check with the unnecessary joint payment (to the mortgagee).

IV. SPECIFIC EXPERTISE TO RENDER THESE EXPERT OPINIONS[4]

(i) Specific Expertise as to These Opinions

In connection with these opinions, I have drawn on my expertise (i) as summarized below and (ii) as set forth in my Curriculum Vitae, attached.

1A. Expertise As to Insurance Applications and Policies from a Regulatory Perspective. From an educational standpoint, I hold a B.A. in mathematics,[5] a M.Ed. in educational psychology and a J.D. from the University of Illinois and am a member upon examination of the Florida bar along with other state bars, also by examination.

I have had extensive and substantive experience relating directly to insurance applications and policies. As a regulator for eight years in three positions ((i) Assistant Attorney General assigned to the Department of Insurance (Iowa), (ii) First Deputy Commissioner of Insurance and (iii) Commissioner of Insurance), along with my staff, I approved (or disapproved) every word of every phrase of every sentence of every page of every property casualty application and policy used by each of the 1,000 property casualty insurance company doing business in the state, including the type of application and policy[6] at issue in this case.

This regulatory action included applications and policy forms like those at issue in this case. These regulatory positions also included the responsibility to approve (and disapprove, as necessary) proposed premiums to be used in connection with the particular policy form, including premium levels relating to commercial property polices like those at issue here.

While Commissioner, I also served as a member of the Executive Committee of the National Association of Insurance Commissioners ("NAIC"), the nationwide organization of all state insurance commissioners, including Georgia's Commissioner. That organization has responsibilities for establishing model insurance administrative regulations and model statutes for consideration by all of the states.

---

[4] In smarmy fashion, I set out here my qualifications as to this matter. These qualifications should be regard together with my Curriculum Vitae as set forth at Appendix A of this report.

[5] Secondary mathematics education.

[6] That is, a commercial policy (the "Precision Portfolio" policy) at issue.

One of the reasons insurance can be conducted smoothly on a national basis in the U.S. is the comparability of state-by-state insurance laws, many of which originated from NAIC mode laws. While with the NAIC, I served among others on the (i) Commercial Lines Committee, with nationwide jurisdiction over applications and policies such as that at issue here and (ii) on the Casualty Actuarial Committee, which had nationwide jurisdiction over pricing principals for policies such as that at issue here and (iii) finally, I chaired a series of NAIC committees.

1B. *Expertise As to Insurance Applications and Policies from an Insurance Industry Executive and From A Company CEO Perspective* Along these same lines, I served as general counsel and chief lobbyist to the American Academy of Actuaries, Washington D.C. The Academy is the national professional association for actuaries. These professionals establish premium levels for policies such as the policies at issue in this case. In addition, because policy language dictates premium levels, actuaries are also active in determining policy language. While with the profession, I worked with actuaries to establish standards relating to both their work product and professional demeanor.

From 1990 to 1998, I served as President and Chief Executive Officer for the National Council on Compensation Insurance ("NCCI"), New York City and Boca Raton, Florida, a nationwide property casualty industry owned organization with about 1,500 employees with annual revenues of about $150 million that did (and does) business in about 40 states including Georgia, which is also the domiciliary state of NCCI. This means while I served as president and CEO, NCCI was subject to the full authority of the Georgia Office of Insurance Regulation and subject as well to the Georgia Insurance Code as well as the jurisdiction of all Georgia courts, state and federal.

Among my responsibilities at NCCI was (together with my staff) to formulate all workers compensation insurance applications and policy forms as used in our states of operation (about 40 such states). This work included drafting all applications and policy language (tailored to the specific state's Insurance Code) as well as drafting all endorsements and all other policy forms. In addition, my responsibility included gaining state insurance department approval of all such applications and policy forms as a condition precedent to their use as submitted by some 600-property casualty insurance companies.

I am also one of about 400+ certified reinsurance arbitrators (by ARIAS-US) and have sat as an arbitrator on property casualty issues in disputes about policy language between reinsurers and their insurers (like Alfa). I know insurance applications and policies and applications and policy forms.

2A. *Expertise As to Claim Adjustment Duties of Insurance Companies From a Regulatory Perspective.* I have also had significant experience and responsibility in connection with determining and passing judgment on insurers responsibilities in their adjustment of property claims such as those at issue here. In particular, in my three regulatory positions previously described, I had daily responsibility to assure and to hold accountable all of the state's 1,000 property casualty insurers for their claim adjustment obligations. I did so through a series of action steps and tools. The action steps and tools (all of which are likewise used by the GDOI) included the following:

- *Unfair Claims Settlement Act.* Like most every other state (including Georgia), Iowa enacted the model NAIC Unfair Claims Settlement Practices Act ("UCSA") which set forth standards against which the Insurance Commissioner could pass judgment on a property insurer's claims settlement practices. As Commissioner and as First Deputy and earlier as Assistant Attorney General assigned to the Department, I had daily responsibility to enforce this act and assure all insurance companies were in compliance with the act. That was the same act as adopted in Georgia in substantially similar form and enforced on regular basis by the GDOI.

- *NAIC Market Conduct Examiners Handbook.* In addition to the standards set out in the UCSA, as Commissioner, I had as an available tool, the NAIC Market Conduct Examiners Handbook ("Examiners Handbook" or "Handbook"). This Handbook sets forth standards to assess insurer claim settlement behavior and is used by every department of insurance in the United States including Georgia. The standards have been universally agreed to by all of the nation's Commissioners of Insurance as adopted formally by them through the NAIC. The claim settlement standards of the Handbook are universally recognized as appropriate standards against which to judge insurer claim behavior.

- *Market Conduct Examination.* On a regular basis, my agency conducted Market Conduct Examinations of property insurers utilizing the Examiners Handbook to determine whether in fact the target insurer was meeting all of their claim settlement obligations. This action entailed physically going into the insurers claim operations and studying claim files to determine any errant action or inappropriate claim settlement behavior. As further discussed below, errant insurers were warned, disciplined and prosecuted as required.

- *Complaints From the Public.* On a daily basis, my Department received incoming consumer complaints as to insurance company claim settlement practices. This division was staffed by Department lawyers who resolved the individual complaint but equally important, those lawyers also determined whether an insurer evidenced unacceptable claim settlement practices. That is to say, staff lawyers determined whether the incoming consumer complaints in fact constituted a red flag as to the insurance company's potential behavior across the board.

- *Prosecution.* To the extent insurer behavior required formal action (whether a result of complaints from the public or a result of Department investigation through a Market Conduct Examination), my Department prosecuted such insurers under the state's civil Administrative Procedures Act. In connection with such prosecutions, I served in various capacities during my eight years as a regulator as (i) prosecutor (as Assistant Attorney General), (ii) as the decision maker as to whether to initiate prosecution in the first instance and (iii) as the

Administrative Law Judge ("ALJ")[7] who presided over the prosecution and defense of the case and entered findings of fact and conclusions of law as to insurer claim settlement practices. I have served as an ALJ in scores of such cases where the insurer's claim settlement practices in property claim settlement matters were the primary issue and entered final decisions in such matters.

2B. Expertise As to Claim Adjustment Duties of Insurance Companies From the Perspective of an Industry Executive. In addition to my experience as a regulator, as reflected above, I have had specific industry experience (in other positions) as to insurer claim settlement practices. Some of those positions included the following:

- *CEO of a Major US Insurance Organization, Regulated Throughout the US: Domiciled in Florida; President and Chief Executive Office of the National Council on Compensation Insurance (NCCI, Boca Raton, Florida), 1990 – 1998.* I referenced above, under policy expertise, my experience at NCCI. In addition to exposure as to insurance policy forms, this same NCCI experience also provided significant background as to insurer claim settlement obligations.

  NCCI. Claim Settlement. In addition and relevant to this case, NCCI had a vested interest in member insurer claim practices in that the industry's reputation for fair underwriting and claim settlement practices ultimately impacted regulatory attitudes toward NCCI's premium approval process.

  NCCI. Industry Standards of Practice. While President and CEO of NCCI, I visited and physically toured and reviewed in excess of 400 insurance companies and gained direct exposure to the procedures and processes and standard industry practices of the U.S. insurance community and its claim settlement practices. I have had extensive exposure to insurer practices and procedures.

- *General Counsel and Director of Government Relations to the American Academy of Actuaries (Washington D.C.), 1980 – 1983.* I served as General Counsel and Director of Government Relations for the American Academy of Actuaries, including advising on admissions, discipline, federal antitrust and general corporate law. I represented the 15,000-member professional organization before Congress (e.g., Senate Committees on Banking, Commerce, Finance and Labor, and House committees on Education, Labor, Energy, and Ways and Means) and the various federal regulatory agencies.

  The Academy is the professional organization of actuaries and includes qualified actuaries from all disciplines and all forms of insurers. Academy members included affiliation with virtually every commercial property insurance company in America. Such actuaries had duties relating to policy language and policy pricing. The Academy's Board of Directors was likewise made up of leading insurance company executives from such property companies.

---

[7] Then known as the "Hearing Officer".

10

150

- *Attorney in Private Practice.* As an attorney in private practice, I represented a number of agent and insurer interests and became familiar with applicable regulatory and industry claim settlement standards of practice. Those interests included the position of Iowa Counsel to the National Association of Independent Insurers.

  Attorney in Private Practice: Commercial Property Insurance Issues. Those interests also included intimate involvement with commercial property insurance, as counsel to the:

  > Professional Insurance Agents of Iowa (property casualty insurance agents);

  > Iowa Association of Life Underwriters (life, health and annuity insurance agents); and

  > The Property Casualty Insurance Association of America ("PCIAA"; I served as Iowa Counsel to this trade group), the trade association of smaller stock property casualty insurers.

  Specific duties as counsel at both the Professional Insurance Agents of Iowa (who sold, among other coverages, commercial property insurance) and the Iowa Association of Life Underwriters (life, health and annuity insurance agents) included in-depth familiarity with commercial property insurers, their agents and their claim settlement practices. Specific duties at the PCIAA included daily counsel to member insurers as to their claim settlement duties.

In sum, I know insurer claim settlement duties, whether in Georgia or elsewhere.

(ii) More General Expertise

In addition to the more specific expertise set out above, among other positions and experiences, the following experience were also particularly relevant to this report and my opinions:

11

A. Formal Education.

- **1. Bachelors Degree in Mathematics.** I hold a bachelors degree in secondary mathematics education from the University of Northern Iowa;

- **2. Masters Degree in Psychology.** I hold a masters degree in educational psychology from the University of Hawaii; and

- **3. Juris Doctor's Degree.** I hold a J.D. degree from the University of Illinois.

B. Licensure and Certification.

- **4. Certified Reinsurance Arbitrator.** I am certified by ARIAS as one of about 250 U.S. certified reinsurance arbitrators;

- **5. Admitted to Practice Law.** I am licensed and admitted to practice law upon examination in the states of Iowa, Illinois and Florida; and

- **6. Admitted to Practice before the U.S. Supreme Court.** I am also admitted to practice before the U.S. Supreme Court.

C. Insurance Expert.

- **7. Expert Witness.** I have served as an expert witness in several cases throughout the U.S. and have been qualified at trial as an expert witness in about 15 to 20 states.

- **8. Insurance Consultant to the U.S. Attorney.** By way of example of my various assignments, I am currently retained by the U.S. Attorney, the Middle District of Florida, as an insurance consultant in a complex civil insurance matter.

- **9. Insurance Consultant to the U.S. Department of Justice.** Similarly, I have also been retained by the U.S. Department of Justice as an insurance consultant in a complex insurance case.

- **10. Expert Witness: the United States Air Force.** I am currently serving as an expert witness for the United States Air Force in a complex CGL case.

- **11. Expert Witness: on Behalf of Various Departments of Insurance.** I have also been retained as an expert witness by the: (i) Florida Office of Insurance Regulation and have testified on their behalf in Florida state and federal court,[*] and (ii) the Arizona Department of Insurance and testified on

---

[*] I am scheduled to so testify April 5, 2010.

12

EXHIBIT A-1

their behalf. Similarly, I have testified as an insurance expert before the following state Departments of Insurance: Florida, Oklahoma, South Dakota, Texas and Nevada.

D. Industry Background: Reinsurance Arbitrator.

- **12. Reinsurance Arbitrator: Commercial Property[9] Cases. November 2003 to Present.** My background includes extensive exposure to the various reinsurance mechanisms and relationships. Along these same lines and as indicated above, I am a certified ARIAS-US reinsurance arbitrator (see immediately below) and have sat as an arbitrator in cases between commercial property insurers and their reinsurers. The relevance of this experience to this case is that reinsurers have substantial influence on the underwriting standards of commercial property insurers.

As of November 2003, I was certified by AIDA Reinsurance and Insurance Arbitration Society, United States ("ARIAS-US") as an arbitrator for reinsurance and insurance matters. Today, there are about 400+ individuals so certified by ARIAS in the United States.

ARIAS-US certifies knowledgeable and reputable professionals for service as panel members in reinsurance and insurance arbitration matters. The organization's criteria for certification are as follows:

- 10 years of significant specialization in the insurance/reinsurance industry;

- Arbitration experience – must have completed appropriate credited ARIAS seminars;

- A member in good standing of ARIAS-US;

- Appropriate endorsement from existing members.

E. Industry Background in General

- **13. CEO of a Major US Insurance Organization, Regulated Throughout the US; President and Chief Executive Office of the National Council on Compensation Insurance (NCCI), 1990 – 1998.** NCCI is one of the larger and more pervasive U.S. insurance organizations. During my tenure as President and CEO, NCCI had (and continues to have) responsibility to accurately price and file pricing for some $12 - $15 billion of workers compensation insurance in 39 states throughout the U.S. NCCI prepared proposed premium filings for regulators to approve by extracting key data

---

[9] The Alfa policy at issue is a commercial property policy (which provided other coverages as well).

from its 600 member insurance companies and then used that data to project necessary premium changes. NCCI accomplished this mission through some 1,000 employees of which approximately 600 were professionals, and had an annual revenues of $140 million.

Insurance Program. As CEO, I had daily exposure and responsibilities to the U.S. workers compensation program as administered by the various states, which constitutes one of the largest property casualty insurance programs in the world with some 100 million worker lives insured (in addition, of course, other important coverages are provided through workers compensation, most notably life insurance, wage replacement and medical coverage).

Applications and Policy Forms. In addition and relevant to this case, NCCI promulgated most all application forms and policy forms used by the workers compensation insurance industry in Georgia and throughout most all of the United States. I am very familiar with the requirements relating to application forms and policy forms in the various states including Georgia.

Industry Standards of Practice. While President and CEO of NCCI, I visited and physically toured and reviewed in excess of 400 insurance companies and gained direct exposure to the procedures and processes and standard industry practices of the U.S. insurance community and its underwriting and claim settlement practices. I have had extensive exposure to insurer practices and procedures.

Licensed to do Business in Georgia: Familiar with Georgia's Regulatory Scheme. While CEO of NCCI, it was (and remains) licensed to do business in Georgia as to that state's workers compensation rate making and underwriting organization. In that capacity, my company, NCCI, was subject to licensure by the Georgia Department of Insurance and was subject as well to the regulatory scrutiny of the Department as well as being subject to all applicable provisions of the Georgia Insurance Code. NCCI was also subject to state and federal jurisdiction as to Georgia. As such, I am familiar with the regulatory and statutory scheme that is brought to bear on insurance in the state.

- 14. **General Counsel and Director of Government Relations to the American Academy of Actuaries (Washington D.C.), 1980 – 1983.** I served as General Counsel and Director of Government Relations for the American Academy of Actuaries, including advising on admissions, discipline, federal antitrust and general corporate law. I represented the 10,000-member professional organization before Congress (e.g., Senate Committees on Banking, Commerce, Finance and Labor, and House committees on Education, Labor, Energy, and Ways and Means) and the various federal regulatory agencies.

14

Commercial Property Insurance Companies. The Academy is the professional organization of actuaries and includes qualified actuaries from all disciplines and all forms of insurers. Academy members included affiliation with virtually every commercial property insurance company in America. The Academy's Board of Directors was likewise made up of leading insurance company executives from such companies.

- **15. Risk Metrics Corporation.** I co-founded this information company in 1998. Risk Metrics (including Datalister, Inc.) gathers and sells public data relating to workers compensation to a wide range of insurance oriented customers, including insurance agents. Within the last few years, I have sold my interest in this corporation.

- **16. Attorney in Private Practice.** As an attorney in private practice, I represented a number of agent and insurer interests and became familiar with applicable regulatory and industry standards of practice, including custom and practice relating to policy applications and policy forms. Those interests included the position of Iowa Counsel to the Property Casualty Insurers Association of America.

  Commercial Property Insurance Issues. Those interests also included intimate involvement with commercial property insurance, as counsel to the:

  Professional Insurance Agents of Iowa and

  Iowa Association of Life Underwriters (life, health and annuity insurance agents).

  Specific duties as counsel at both the Professional Insurance Agents of Iowa (who sold, among other coverages, commercial property insurance) and the Iowa Association of Life Underwriters (life, health and annuity insurance agents) included in-depth familiarity with commercial property insurers, their agents and their claim settlement practices.

F. Regulatory

- **17. Commissioner of Insurance, Iowa 1986 – 1990.** As Insurance Commissioner appointed by Governor Terry Branstad in July 1986, I was responsible for the regulatory oversight of all insurance companies, agents and brokers authorized to conduct business in the state of Iowa. My agency was responsible for solvency oversight, insurance company examinations, financial and accounting matters of insurance companies, consumer protection, agent and broker licensing, and oversight of commercial property insurance company practices, including policy application forms and policy forms themselves as well as claim settlement practices. In particular, that oversight included the responsibility of overseeing practices of commercial property insurer claim settlement practices. In addition, I oversaw the state regulation of the securities industry with Iowa's Superintendent of Securities reporting directly to me.

Regulatory Oversight: Commercial Property Insurer Practices Including Policy Applications.   In addition, as Insurance Commissioner, my responsibilities included oversight over the education, licensing, discipline and general supervision of all commercial property insurance companies in the state.[10]   I am very familiar with the responsibilities and applicable obligations that come to bear upon commercial property insurance companies including their applications and policy forms.

Regulatory Oversight: Commercial Property Insurance Application Process and Underwriting and Claims Settlement.   As Insurance Commissioner, I also had day-to-day responsibility to assure that all underwriting and applications and policy forms and policy issuance practices and claim settlement practices carried out by commercial property insurance companies doing business in the state met their duties, obligations and statutory and regulatory responsibilities as they underwrote policies and settled cases.

Financial Examination of Commercial Property Insurance Companies. As Insurance Commissioner, I directed and oversaw the examination of all insurance companies authorized to do business in the State of Iowa. Those examinations included focus on both financial matters (so called triennial examinations of insurers – of which well over 100 such examinations were conducted while I was Commissioner) and examinations of specific complaints about insurers (so called Market Conduct Examinations - well over 50 such exams were conducted while I was Commissioner).

Market Conduct Examinations of Commercial Property Insurer Claim Settlement Practices. Market Conduct Examinations focused on marketplace issues such as those at issue in this case, specifically examining commercial property insurance companies as to compliance with their application processes. Concurrent with such exams, I personally reviewed and approved the final Examination Reports before they were issued. In addition, in many of these instances, I visited the subject commercial property insurer before the Examination Report was issue, including walking the floors of such insurance companies – reviewing their effected operations first hand.

Prosecution of Commercial Property Insurance Companies. As Insurance Commissioner, I employed a full time team of lawyers who fielded consumer complaints relating to all areas of commercial property insurance company operations. Indeed, many of these complaints, as well as results of Market Conduct Examinations, resulted in formal action under the state's

---

[10]   Who held an insurance agent's license with authority to sell commercial property insurance.

Administrative Procedures Act. From time to time, I served as the Hearing Officer as to such matters.

Major Insurance State. Iowa has about 1,000 authorized property and casualty insurance companies, many of whom write commercial property insurance and over 500 life insurance companies and an unusually large number of domestic insurance companies and as such, insurance regulation in that state is a serious job.

Familiarity with Georgia's Insurance Regulation. As Insurance Commissioner in Iowa with interaction with Georgia regulators, as a member of the NAIC with frequent interaction with the Georgia Department of Insurance and as CEO of NCCI, where we were domiciled in Georgia and licensed to conduct business in Georgia by the Georgia Department of Insurance, I am familiar with the regulatory scheme in place in Georgia.

- **18. National Association of Insurance Commissioners (NAIC), 1986 – 1990.** Concurrent with my service as Iowa Insurance Commissioner, I served as a member of the NAIC. The NAIC is an organization of the Insurance Commissioners of all 50 states and meets quarterly in locations throughout the U.S. to consider and evaluate national insurance issues. Further, the organization is professionally staffed with more than one hundred personnel. The organization is based in Kansas City, Missouri. The NAIC considers all major insurance issues and then promulgates model insurance laws and regulations, which are then routinely (but optionally) adopted at the individual state level.

NAIC Chairmanships – Chairman of the Midwest Zone. I was elected by my fellow Insurance Commissioners from the Midwest Zone (composed of the Midwest states, constituting about one quarter of all of the states) to provide leadership and representation of the Midwest before the balance of the states. This position included a position on the Executive Committee of the NAIC as well as major responsibilities relating to the assignment of states (and their related examiners) to specific examinations, both triennial and Market Conduct.

NAIC Leadership: Member of the Executive Committee. I also served as an elected member of the Executive Committee of the NAIC, the body that served as the steering committee of the organization, providing leadership between full membership meetings and providing recommendations to the full membership as to complex or politically charged issues within the organization.

Other NAIC Chairmanships: I also served in a number of NAIC capacities including Chairman of the Financial Services and Insurance Regulation Task Force.

17

Member: Commercial Lines Committee. Among the many committees, I chaired or was a member of, was the Commercial Lines Committee, which had responsibility to set national policy with respect to commercial lines insurers and their products such as property insurance.

In addition, my service on the following NAIC Committees was also helpful in this regard:

- Member, the Blanks Committee
- Member, Guarantee Fund Committee
- Member, Rehabilitator and Liquidators Committee
- Member, Casualty Actuarial Committee
- Member, Commercial Lines Committee
- Member, Valuation of Securities Committee,
- Member, International Insurance Relations Committee
- Member, Accounting Practices and Procedures Committee and
- Member, State and Federal Legislative Committee.

NAIC Chairmanships – Chair of the Life Insurance Committee: Underwriting Issues. As a member of the NAIC, I served as both Vice Chairman and Chairman of the NAIC Life Insurance Committee. The charge of this Committee was oversight over all issues relating to life insurance products (including illustrations) as well as commercial property insurers, including practices such as underwriting.

NAIC Chairmanships: Chair of the Universal Life Insurance Task Force. In addition to chairing the Life Insurance Committee, I also chaired the Universal Commercial property Insurance Task Force.

NAIC Chairmanships: Chair of the Life Insurance Product Development Task Force. I also chaired the Life Insurance Product Development Task Force. While chairman of this task force, I led the development of model disclosure statements for universal and indeterminate premium life products designed to assist consumers in their comparison of different types of interest sensitive life insurance products.

Ongoing Regulatory Involvement. In the years since leaving the regulatory ranks, I have continued to be closely involved with the NAIC and the regulatory community. As President and CEO of NCCI, I was in regular attendance at meetings of the NAIC and continue to attend these meetings and to be actively engaged with the regulatory process. Included in this attendance were my observations at the NAIC of the regulation of the commercial property industry.

- **19. First Deputy Commissioner of Insurance, Iowa 1976 – 1978.** As First Deputy Insurance Commissioner, I was responsible for the regulatory oversight of all insurance companies, agents and brokers authorized to conduct business in the state of Iowa. I was responsible for solvency oversight, insurance company examinations, financial and accounting matters of insurance companies, consumer protection, agent and broker licensing, and oversight of commercial property insurance company practices, including their application and policy issuance processes and their claim settlement practices. In particular, that oversight included the responsibility of overseeing practices of commercial property insurer claim settlement practices.

Regulatory Oversight: Commercial Property Insurer Practices: Applications. In addition, as First Deputy Insurance Commissioner, my responsibilities included oversight over the education, licensing, discipline and general supervision of all commercial property insurance companies in the state. I am very familiar with the responsibilities and applicable obligations that come to bear upon commercial property insurance companies, including their obligations as to applications and policy issuance.

Regulatory Oversight: Commercial Property Insurance: Applications and Underwriting. As First Deputy Insurance Commissioner, I also had day-to-day responsibility to assure that all claim settlement practices carried out by commercial property insurance companies doing business in the state met their duties, obligations and statutory and regulatory responsibilities as they settled cases.

Financial Examination of Commercial Property Insurance Companies. As First Deputy Insurance Commissioner, I directed and oversaw the examination of all insurance companies authorized to do business in the State of Iowa, including commercial property insurers. Those examinations included focus on both financial matters (so called triennial examinations of insurers – of which well over 50 such examinations were conducted while I was First Deputy Insurance Commissioner) and examinations of specific complaints about insurers (so called Market Conduct Examinations - well over 50 such exams were conducted while I was First Deputy Insurance Commissioner; see the discussion that follows).

Market Conduct Examinations of Commercial Property Insurer Claim Settlement Practices. Market Conduct Examinations focused on marketplace issues such as those at issue in this case, specifically examining commercial property insurance companies as to compliance with their application and policy issuance and claim settlement practices. Concurrent with such exams, along with the Commissioner, I personally reviewed the final Examination Reports before they were issued. In addition, in many of these instances, I visited the subject commercial property insurer before the Examination Report was issue, reviewing their effected operations first hand.

Prosecution of Commercial Property Insurance Companies. As First Deputy Insurance Commissioner, I oversaw a full time team of lawyers who fielded consumer complaints relating to all areas of commercial property insurance company operations. Indeed, many of these complaints, as well as results of Market Conduct Examinations, resulted in formal action under the state's Administrative Procedures Act. From time to time, I served as the Hearing Officer as to such matters.

- **20.   Iowa Assistant Attorney General Assigned to the Insurance Department**, 1975-1976; serving as the Department's General Counsel. As Assistant Attorney General, I had departmental prosecutorial responsibilities for violations of the Insurance Code under the state's APA act including those committed by commercial property insurance companies. The Attorney General responsibility also included issuing Attorney General Opinions as to the construction of insurance laws and regulations.

- **21. Legal Counsel to House of Representatives.** As legal counsel to the Iowa House of Representative (1975 session), I provided counsel on all relevant caucus issues and provided the following support:

    - Researched pending legislation,

    - Prepared memorandums in support of proposed legislation,

    - Provided legal advice, and

    - Participated in bill drafting, including that relating to commercial property insurance.

- **22. Lecturer at the Bar Review School, authoring and delivering the Insurance Course** to students studying for the Iowa Bar Exam (from about 1985- 1991). I was invited to provide the insurance content review material and lecture for the insurance section of the bar review course in Iowa. Included in this lecture was extensive law applicable to the interpretation and construction of laws and regulations applicable to commercial property insurance companies, including their application and policy issuance practices and their underwriting practices. I authored this material and provided this lecture to students studying to pass the bar for about six years, until accepting the position of President and CEO of NCCI in Florida.

- **23.   Administrative Assistant to the U.S. Congress.** I served as an Administrative Assistant to the U.S. Congress in Washington D.C. to an Iowa

Congressman for about a year. Among others, I participated in legislative drafting of insurance and reinsurance legislation.

Signed electronically and dated this 22st day of March, 2010. *aNd Signed Personally*

William D. Hager
William D. Hager

UNITED STATES DISTRICT COURT
FOR THE MIDDLE DISTRICT IN GEORGIA
MACON DIVISION

UNITED STATES OF AMERICA	)	
	)	
Respondent	)	CRIMINAL NO. 5:07-CR-00077-CAR
	)	
vs.	)	
	)	CIVIL NO. 5:10CV90085
ONSLOW D. ROSS.	)	
	)	
Petitioner	)	
	)	

STATE OF GEORGIA

COUNTY OF DEKALB

AFFIDAVIT OF KENNETH C. GRIM

Personally appeared before me the undersigned officer duly authorized to administer oaths came Kenneth C. Grim who, after being duly sworn, states on oath his personal knowledge as follows:

1.

My name is Kenneth C. Grim. I have personal knowledge of the facts as alleged in the following documents, which I have reviewed:

    a.   Current owner title search on property at 2515 Rocky Creek Road, Macon, Bibb County, Georgia performed by Charles W. Field on April 28, 2010.

    b.   Current owner title search on property at 5555 Bethesda Avenue, Macon, Bibb County, performed by Charles W. Field on April 28, 2010.

    c.   Secretary of State of Georgia public access corporation records.

    d.   Georgia Superior Court Clerks' Cooperative Authority subscription access deed records.

2.

I am of legal age and under no legal disability. I am an attorney-at-law licensed to practice law in the State of Georgia since 1995. This Affidavit is given for use as evidence in connection with the above-styled action and in accordance with O.C.G.A. § 9-11-9.1(a).

3.

My residence is in Sandy Springs, Georgia, and I am an attorney with the law firm of Shafritz & Dean, LLC. I received my B.A. from Emory University and received my J.D. from Georgia State University Law School. During my career as an attorney, I served as a Title Examiner for Gwinnett Title & Abstract Services managing commercial and residential title research and Resolution Trust Corporation disposition of Savings & Loan assets. I worked as a Title Examiner for two years for Storey & Obenschain, LLC. where I performed commercial and residential title searches, searched personal property records, drafted commitments and title insurance policies, and cleared exceptions with title insurance underwriters. As Associate General Counsel for Huddle House, Inc. I negotiated and drafted land, building and equipment leases, franchise agreements, collateral agreements and related documentation for a period of six years. Subsequently I provided private counsel related to business mergers and acquisitions and negotiating and drafting commercial and residential real estate transactions for two years. As Senior Regional Counsel and Assistant Vice President for United General Title Insurance Company for four years, I oversaw all company an agent legal duties in a five-state territory, processed underwriting inquiries and authorized coverage exceeding agent limits, resolved claims and managed outside counsel for claims and litigation, conducted audits of underwriting procedures, supervised agent regulatory compliance and training, and coordinated anti-fraud activities. I currently work as an attorney for Shaftitz & Dean, LLC. where I have practiced for the last two years.

4.

Based on the foregoing documentation I have reviewed, it is my expert opinion that the tract of real property, which will be known for the purposes of this affidavit as the "Rocky Creek Property", is commonly known by the street address 2515 Rocky Creek Road. Macon, Georgia, has a legal description as follows:

All that tract or parcel of land lying and being in the Godfrey District in Land Lot 122, and being more particularly described as follows: Being a part of Lot 1 as shown on plat of Sunnyside, made by R.W. Cowan, C.E. on March 2, 1960 and recorded in Plat Book 19, Folio 49, beginning at a point where the dividing line between Lots 1 and 2 intersects the north side of Rocky Creek Road and running thence in a northerly direction along said dividing line a distance of two hundred (200.0) feet; thence angle right and parallel with Rocky Creek Road a distance of two hundred ten (210.0) feet; thence in a southerly direction and parallel with the dividing line between Lots 1 and 2 to the north side of Rocky Creek Road two hundred (200.0) feet; thence in a westerly direction along the north side of Rocky Creek Road a distance of two hundred ten (210.0) feet to the point of beginning.

5.

Based on the foregoing documentation I have reviewed, it is my expert opinion that the tract of real property, which will be known for the purposes of this affidavit as the "Bethesda Avenue Property", is commonly known by the street address 5555 Bethesda Avenue, Macon, Georgia, and has a legal description as follows:

> All that tract or parcel of land lying and being in Bibb County, Georgia known and distinguished as Lots 21, 22, 23, 24, 25, 26 and a part of Lot 1 in Block A of Sunnyside, according to a plat of record in Plat Book 22, Page 45, Clerk's office, Bibb Superior Court. Said tract of land is more particularly described as follows:

> Beginning at a point on the south side of Anderson Drive, where the same is intersected by the line dividing Lots 20 and 21 in Block A of said subdivision; thence south along the line dividing said lots 20 and 21 a distance of 287 feet; thence east along the rear lines of Lots 21, 22, 23 and 24 a distance of 490 feet; thence south along the line dividing Lots 1 and 2 a distance of 92.9 feet; thence in an easterly direction across Lot 1 to Shela Drive a distance of 210 feet to a point which is 200 feet north of Rocky Creek Road; thence north along Shela Drive a distance of 318.5 feet to Anderson Drive; thence west along Anderson Drove a distance of 610 feet to the point of beginning.

6.

It is my expert legal opinion that the Bethesda Avenue Property and the Rocky Creek Property are two separate and distinct parcels of real property, with the Rocky Creek Property being situated to the south of the Bethesda Avenue Property and adjacent to the same, with no apparent overlaps in the deed descriptions.

7.

The Bethesda Avenue Property was granted by deed to Reaching Souls Cathedral of Praise Apostolic Church, Inc., a Georgia Corporation, by Bethesda Avenue Baptist Church on December 31, 2003, by deed recorded January 23, 2004 at Deed Book 6073, Page 70, Bibb County Superior Court records.

8.

The Rocky Creek Property was granted by deed to C B & T Bank of Middle Georgia by Bethesda Avenue Baptist Church, Inc. on April 8, 2006, by deed recorded April 12, 2006 at Deed Book 7023, Page 50, Bibb County Superior Court records.

9.

The Rocky Creek Property was granted by deed to Reaching Souls Cathedral of Praise Apostolic Church, Inc. a Georgia Corporation, by C.B. & T Bank of Middle Georgia in September 27, 2007, by deed recorded October 11, 2007 at Deed Book 7657, Page 86, Bibb County Superior Court Records.

10.

Based on the foregoing chain of title, it is clear that the two properties referenced herein were treated as separate and distinct properties prior to December 11, 2006.

11.

The Bethesda Road Property was subjected to a Security Deed dated December 31, 2003 by Reaching Souls Cathedral of Praise to C B & T Bank of Middle Georgia, recorded at Deed Book 6073, Page 73, on December 31, 2003, Bibb County Superior Court records. This Deed to Secure Debt has been cancelled and released of record.

12.

The Bethesda Road Property was also subjected to a Secondary Deed to Secure Debt dated December 31, 2003 by Reaching Souls Cathedral of Praise Apostolic Church, Inc. to Bethesda Avenue Baptist Church, Inc., recorded at Deed Book 6073, Page 88, on December 31, 2003, Bibb County Superior Court Records. This Deed to Secure Debt has been cancelled and released of record.

13.

The Rocky Creek Property was at no time in the public record conveyed to C B & T Bank of Middle Georgia as security for a loan.

14.

Based upon the foregoing documentation that I have reviewed, it is my expert legal opinion that the Rocky Creek Property is free and clear of Deeds to Secure Debt or other liens and was free and clear of any liens in May of 2005 when the roof on the building at that property collapsed. Based upon the foregoing documentation that I have reviewed, it is my expert legal opinion that C B & T did not have any interest giving them a right to any insurance proceeds on 2515 Rocky Creek Rd in May 2005.

15.

Based on the aforementioned review, it is my expert legal opinion that the Bethesda Road Property is encumbered by a Deed to Secure Debt granted to Foundation Capital Resources, Inc. dated December 11, 2006, recorded on December 16, 2006, at Deed Book 7327, Page 259, Bibb County Superior Court records.

[SIGNATURES ON FOLLOWING PAGE]

FURTHER AFFIANT SAYETH NAUGHT

Sworn to before me
this 24th day of November, 2010.

Kenneth C. Grim
Georgia Bar No. 312440

Notary Public
My commission expires:
[NOTARY SEAL]

Hutcheson

100 Gross Crescent Circle
Fort Oglethorpe, Georgia 30741

706.858.2000

Fax Transmittal

Date _____ 11-29-11 _____

To:

Name _____ Fuller, McKay - Attn: Julie _____

Fax # _____ (404) 592-6225 _____

From:

Employee Name _____ Donna - Patient Accounts Dept. _____

Fax # _____ 706. 858. 2844 _____

Phone # _____ 706. 858. 2304 _____

Number of pages including this cover page _____ 2 _____

Message:

_____ - sent at patient's request - _____

Form 1545 (BACK)

Nov. 21. 2011, 8:46AM
CINCINNATI, OH 45263-8019

No. 4416   P. 2/3

PATIENT STATEMENT

MED. REC./WARD	STATEMENT DATE
84064570/401	11/28/1

CHECK NUMBER	PAYMENT AMT

FOR PROPER POSTING
PLEASE WRITE IN CHECK
NUMBER AND AMOUNT PAID

84064570-401-6517

SAMUEL L RAYMOND
8192 LAKE RD
TUNNEL HILL GA 30755

PLEASE WRITE YOUR ACCOUNT NUMBER ON YOUR CHECK.
MAKE PAYABLE IN U.S. DOLLARS TO:

EMERGENCY COVERAGE CORP.
PO BOX 635019
CINCINNATI, OH 45263-6019

PATIENT NAME: SAMUEL L RAYMOND

TO PAY BY CREDIT CARD, COMPLET
AND SIGN THE OTHER SIDE OF THIS STATEMENT

PHYSICIAN SERVICES RENDERED AT HUTCHESON MEDICAL CENTER
PAYMENTS AND INSURANCE INFORMATION MAILED SEVEN DAYS
PRIOR TO THE ABOVE STATEMENT DATE MAY NOT YET APPEAR.

TAXPAYER ID:	62-1130266
BILLING INQUIRIES:	1-888-952-6772

HOURS OF OPERATION: MONDAY - FRIDAY 8AM TO 8PM & SATURDAY 10AM TO 3PM ET
PROVIDE INSURANCE INFO OR PAY BY CREDIT CARD AT WWW.TEAM-HEALTH.COM/BILLING

DATE	CODE	DESCRIPTION	PROVIDER	CHARGE	PAYMENT/ADJ
12/08/10	99284	EMERGENCY DEPT VISIT - 99284		615.00	
97205274	858.0	NABSOUR MD, PAUL A / YELLIOTT PA-C, BRANT			

PHYSICIAN CHARGES ARE NOT INCLUDED IN THE FACILITY BILL

| ACCOUNT NUMBER | 84064570/401 | STATEMENT DATE | 11/28/11 | 1D10 | TOTAL NOW DUE ▶ | 615.0 |

LAW OFFICES
DANIEL, LAWSON, TUGGLE & JERLES, LLP
913 MAIN STREET
P.O. BOX 89
PERRY GEORGIA 31069-0089

TOM W. DANIEL
ROBERT T. TUGGLE III
WILLIAM K. JERLES JR
ROBERT E. LAWSON

HUGH LAWSON IV
(1941-1988)

February 2, 2006

TELEPHONE 478-987-8922
TELECOPIER 478-987-7622
www.dlt.com
email dlt@dlt.com

DAVID P. HELMERT SR
(1880-1963)

CERTIFIED MAIL #7005 0390 0003 0214 6585
RETURN RECEIPT REQUESTED
Pastor Onslow Ross, Chief Executive Officer
Reaching Souls Cathedral of Praise
5555 Bethesda Avenue
Macon, GA 31206-4470

RE   Note and Security Deed to CB&T Bank of Middle Georgia.
5555 Bethesda Avenue

Dear Pastor Ross:

Our law firm has been employed by CB&T Bank of Middle Georgia to commence foreclosure proceedings against the above referenced property immediately. This is due to **Reaching Souls Cathedral of Praise** being in default under the terms of the note and Security Deed. Accordingly, the entire amount of the outstanding balance of principal and interest of the loan has been and is hereby declared immediately due and payable. This letter is demand for immediate payment of $117,717.07.

This letter is further notice that CB&T Bank of Middle Georgia intends to enforce the provisions relative to the payment of attorney's fees as provided in the note and O.C.G.A. §13-1-11. If the total principal and interest is not paid within ten (10) days from the receipt of this letter, attorney's fees in the amount of fifteen (15%) percent of the outstanding principal and interest will also be owed.

The foreclosure sale is scheduled for the first Tuesday in March, 2006 on the steps of the courthouse door of Bibb County, Georgia. Enclosed is a copy of the notice of sale which will be submitted to the publisher of the legal newspaper for publication for four (4) consecutive weeks prior to the sale date.

Very truly yours,

Robert T. Tuggle III

cc: Mr. Steve Williams

NOTICE OF SALE

Because of default under the terms of the deed to secure debt executed by

REACHING SOULS CATHEDRAL OF PRAISE to CB&T BANK OF MIDDLE GEORGIA,

dated December 31, 2003, and recorded in Deed Book 6073, pages 73-82, Clerk's Office,

Bibb Superior Court, the undersigned CB&T BANK OF MIDDLE GEORGIA, pursuant to

the power of sale contained in said security deed, will, on the first Tuesday in March 2006,

during the legal hours of sale, at the courthouse door in Macon, Bibb County, Georgia, sell

at public outcry to the highest and best bidder for cash the property described in said deed,

to-wit:

All that tract or parcel of land lying and being in Bibb County, Georgia, known and distinguished as Lots 21,22,23,24,25,,26, and a part of Lot 1 in Block A of Sunnyside, according to a plat of record in Plat 22, Folio 45, Clerk's Office Bibb Superior Court. Said tract of land is more particularly described as follow:

Beginning at a point on the south said of Anderson Drive, where the same is intersected by the line dividing Lots 20 and 21 in Block A, of said subdivision; thence south along the line dividing said Lots 20 and 21 a distance of 207 feet; thence east along the rear lines of Lots 21, 22, 23, and 24 a distance of 400 feet; thence south along the line to Shela Drive a distance of 210 feet to a point which is 200 feet north of Rocky Creek Road; thence north along Shela Drive a distance of 318.5 fee to Anderson Drive; thence west along Anderson Drive a distance of 610 feet to the point of beginning.

Less and Except that certain property taken in that certain right of way deed dated August 29, 1984, and recorded in Deed Book 1608, Page 797, aforesaid records.

This being a portion of the same property as that conveyed by Warranty Deed from O. L. Cochran, George W. Collins and Joseph B. King, as Trustees of Bethesda Avenue Baptist Church to Bethesda Avenue Baptist Church, Inc., dated November 10, 1961, recorded in Deed Book 886, Page 373, aforesaid records.

Property address known as 5555 Bethesda Ave., Macon GA

Said property will be sold subject to all easements, restrictions and the outstanding ad valorem taxes and/or assessments, if any.

To the best of the undersigned's knowledge and belief, REACHING SOULS CATHEDRAL OF PRAISE is in possession of the property.

A deed will be made by the undersigned to the purchaser at said sale. The proceeds of said sale will be applied as provided in said deed to secure debt.

CB&T BANK OF MIDDLE GEORGIA
as Attorney in fact for
REACHING SOULS CATHEDRAL OF
PRAISE

DANIEL, LAWSON, TUGGLE & JERLES, LLP
POST OFFICE BOX 89
PERRY, GEORGIA 31069

ATTORNEY'S CERTIFICATION

We, Debra G. Gómez and Amy R. Reese, are the attorneys of record for Plaintiff in this case, and this certification is given pursuant to O.C.G.A. § 9-11-65(b). We hereby certify that we have not made any attempts to give notice of the filing of this Complaint, and Request for Injunction, Temporary and Permanent Restraining Order, and Other Relief, to the named Defendant in this action pursuant to O.C.G.A. § 9-11-65(b). It is our opinion that irreparable injury, loss and damage would result to the Plaintiff before this matter would otherwise be heard if advance notice of the filing was provided. A temporary restraining order may be issued without notice pursuant to O.C.G.A. § 9-11-65(b).

This 28ᵗʰ day of February , 2006.

Debra G. Gómez
Debra G. Gómez
Georgia Bar No. 300509
Attorney for Plaintiff

Sworn to and subscribed before
me this 28ᵗʰ day of February , 2006.

Amy R. Reese

NOTARY PUBLIC
My commission expires: 11/4/07

AMY R. REESE
Notary Public
STATE OF GEORGIA
My Comm. Exp. 11/4/07
(SEAL)

Amy R Reese
Amy R Reese
Georgia Bar No. 598145
Attorney for Plaintiff

Sworn to and subscribed before
me this 28ᵗʰ day of February , 2006.
Kimberly Ann Reinhart

NOTARY PUBLIC
My commission expires: 3/15/2009

40

```
 1    affidavit of forgery with the bank that the check was drawn on.

 2    Q    Then which bank, in this case CB&T or Security Bank, had to

 3    end up initially eating the loss?

 4    A    Security Bank did.

 5    Q    And that is what you made demand for payment on?

 6    A    Yes.

 7    Q    Approximately, when did you receive payment from Security

 8    Bank pursuant to that banking policy?

 9    A    In January of '06.  We applied it on February the 2nd, but

10    sometime at the end of January we finally received a check from

11    Security Bank.

12    Q    Now, when did you first learn that there was this issue

13    about the church sitting on two lots of the property in Macon?

14    A    When Rob Tuggle did the first letter, and from there he

15    told us that your lien does not look to be perfected.

16    Q    When is that date, though?

17    A    November the 23rd.

18    Q    Of which year?

19    A    Of 2005.

20    Q    And then you were in court when the Judge read a

21    stipulation of facts about repayment of the loan that Ms. Gomez

22    discussed with you?

23    A    Yes.

24    Q    When was that, when did you receive those funds from an

25    outside source?
```

Handwritten annotations: "1st payment", "2005", "recieved check wrong no mortgage"

February 1, 2006

Ms. Myra Kline
661 Mulberry Street
3rd Floor
District Attorney's Office
Macon, Georgia 31201

Re: Reaching Souls Cathedral of Praise

Dear Ms. Kline:

Security Bank of Bibb County is the victim of the $389,000.00 check forged by Onslow Ross, Pastor of the above-mentioned Church. You currently have this case, however, CB&T Bank actually filed the report.

We became involved in this matter on August 31, 2005, when our customer service representative took for deposit the check endorsed by the Church with CB&Ts endorsement forged. Subsequently, on September 8, 2005 a check was presented and signed by Onslow Ross payable to Willie Ross in the amount of $89,000.00 to purchase two cashiers checks in the amounts of $49,000.00 and $40,000.00. On September 13, 2005, a check was presented and signed by Onslow Ross payable to Rosa Ross in the amount of $100,000.00; on September 19, 2005, a check for $197,000.00 was presented and signed by Onslow Ross to purchase a cashiers check payable to Rosa Ross. On September19, 2005, a check in the amount of $1,656.69 was presented and signed by Onslow Ross to purchase a money order payable to Georgia Power Company. On September 19, 2005, a check was presented payable to cash signed by Onslow Ross for $1,000.00.

The matter began when Alfa Insurance Company issued an insurance draft to Reaching Souls Cathedral of Praise and CB&T bank jointly, on August 23, 2005. CB&T had a lien on the Church and property located at 5555 Bethesda Avenue Macon, Georgia 31206 and the check proceeds should have been submitted to CB&T to reduce their loan balance. When CB&T discovered we had accepted the check for deposit and subsequently allowed Onslow Ross to withdraw the funds, they made demand upon us to reimburse them for the $389,000.00.

I have enclosed all documents pertaining to the matters outlined above, however, if you need anything further, please call me at 478-722-6326, as we desire to pursue this case aggressively.

Additionally, please send me verification that you are pursuing this case on our behalf, and a case number, which I am required to possess for the F.D.I.C. examiners and other regulatory agencies.

I certainly appreciate your cooperation in pursuing this case and bringing Onslow Ross to justice.

Sincerely,

Charles R. Blankenship
Vice President / Security Officer

PLAINTIFF'S
EXHIBIT
13

Shiver & Nelson
Document Investigation Laboratory, Inc.

1903 Lilac Ridge Drive
Woodstock, GA 30189
770-517-6008
Fax: 678-494-9283

Forensic Document Examination Report
Laboratory File No. 08-1958

Prepared For:

Ms. Debra G. Gómez
Gómez Law Group, LLC
1469 Oglethorpe Street
Macon, GA 31208

Re: United States v. Onslow Ross (07-08-056-1MC-01)

A. Documents Submitted for Examination:

Questioned Document:

Q1 –Alfa Mutual Insurance Company check, number D 5503966, made payable to Reaching Soul (sic) Cathedral of Praise and CB&T Bank, dated 8/23/05, in the amount of $389,000.00.

Known writing samples of Mr. Onsiow D. Ross, Ms. Rosa M. Ross, Mr. Undro J. Williams, Ms. Lucile M. Davis, Mr. Joshua R. Jones.

K1(1-79) – Machine copies of various documents bearing the known writing of Mr. Ross, Ms. Ross, Mr. Williams, and Ms. Davis.

K2(1-4) – Machine copies of documents bearing the known writing of Mr. Jones.

    K2(1) – Appeal, dated 1/30/06.

    K2(2) – Performance Summary (Page 4 of 5), undated.

    K2(3) – Group Insurance Application Card, dated 7/20/04.

    K2(4) – Confidential Employee Personal Profile Information Sheet, dated 7/12/04.

K3(1-20) – Handwriting exemplars of Ms. Davis.

Shiver & Nelson Document Investigation Laboratory, Inc.
Report to: Ms. Debra G. Gómez
Lab. File No. 08-1958
Page 2 of 4 Pages

K4 – Machine copy of the Georgia Driver's License of Ms. Davis.

K5(1-20) – Handwriting exemplars of Mr. Williams.

K6 – Machine copy of the Georgia Driver's License of Mr. Williams.

K7(1-20) – Handwriting exemplars of Mr. Ross.

K8 – Machine copy of the Georgia Driver's License of Mr. Ross.

K9(1-19) – Handwriting exemplars of Ms. Ross.

K10 – Machine copy of the Georgia Identification Card of Ms. Ross.

K11(1-5) – Machine copies of checks 514, 515, 516, 517, 518, 519, 521, 522, 523, 527, 528 and 529, on the account of Rosa May Ross, dated from 7/15/2005 to 11/17/05.

B. Determinations Requested:

It was requested that I attempt to determine if Mr. Ross, Ms. Ross, Mr. Williams, Ms. Davis, or Mr. Jones wrote any of the endorsement entries on the back of Document Q1.

C. Opinions:

1. In my professional opinion, Mr. Undre J. Williams wrote the "Reaching Souls Cathedral of Praise" entry on the back of Document Q1.

2. In my professional opinion, it is highly probable that Mr. Ross, Mr. Williams, and Ms. Davis did not write the "CB&T Bamk" (sic) entry on the back of Document Q1.

3. In my professional opinion, Ms. Ross probably did not write the "CB&T Bamk" (sic) entry on the back of Document Q1.

4. No conclusion was reached as to whether Mr. Jones wrote the "CB&T Bamk" (sic) entry on the back of Document Q1.

Shiver & Nelson Document Investigation Laboratory, Inc.
Report to: Ms. Debra G. Gómez
Lab. File No. 08-1958
Page 3 of 4 Pages

D. Observations and Bases for Opinions:

1. Document Q1 is an original document. The questioned endorsement entries were examined macroscopically and microscopically. Two different inks were used to prepare the questioned endorsement entries. The "Reaching Souls Cathedral of Praise" was written using a black non-ballpoint pen ink. The "CB&T Bamk" (sic) entry was written using a blue ballpoint pen ink. No evidence of tracing, simulation (freehand imitation), or disguise was found in the questioned entries.

2. Comparison of the known writing of Mr. Williams disclosed numerous significant similarities and no significant differences. This finding provides the basis for my opinion that Mr. Williams wrote the "Reaching Souls Cathedral of Praise" entry on the back of Document Q1.

3. The questioned "CB&T Bamk" (sic) entry on Document Q1 should logically read "CB&T Bank". While the third letter in "Bamk" appears to be a "m", I cannot rule out the possibility that it is the writer's version of an "n". The letter was compared as both an "n" and an "m". Further, the ampersand in the "CB&T Bamk" entry resembles a cursive capital "S" formation. During my comparison, I compared the questioned ampersand to the known writing samples as both an ampersand and a capital "S".

4. Comparison of the questioned "CB&T Bamk" (sic) entry to the known writing of Mr. Ross, Mr. Williams, and Ms. Davis disclosed numerous significant differences and no significant similarities. These findings provide the basis for my opinion that it is highly probable that Mr. Ross, Mr. Williams, and Ms. Davis did not write the questioned "CB&T Bamk" entry. The primary limitation during my examination was the brevity of the questioned entry.

5. Comparison of the questioned "CB&T Bamk" (sic) entry to the known writing of Ms. Ross disclosed some similarities and also some significant differences. One significant difference is the line quality of questioned entry compared to the line quality of the contemporaneous writing samples of Ms. Ross. The questioned entry displays greater fluency in the writing stroke. In handwriting comparison, significant differences are the controlling factor even in presence of similarities. It is normal for there to be some similarity between the handwriting of different persons. This finding provides the basis for my opinion that Ms. Ross probably did not write the questioned "CB&T Bamk" entry. Limitations during my examination include the brevity of the questioned entry. Other limitations include the issue that the handwriting exemplars were taken post-stroke – Ms. Ross reportedly suffered a stroke in May 2007, which to some degree affected her writing

Shiver & Nelson Document Investigation Laboratory, Inc.
Report to: Ms. Debra G. Gómez
Lab. File No. 08-1958
Page 4 of 4 Pages

ability – and the comparability of the pre-stroke known writing samples. To be fully comparable, known writing samples must contain all of the letterforms used in the questioned writing.

6. The known writing samples of Mr. Jones are not sufficiently comparable to the questioned "CB&T Bamk" entry to support an opinion of authorship. The questioned entry makes use of cursive letterforms whereas the known writing is predominately hand printed. The cursive writing in the known writing of Mr. Jones does not contain a sufficient amount of the letterforms used in the questioned writing. Where comparable letterforms appear, they do not appear in sufficient quantity.

7. The handwriting comparisons described in this report were performed in accordance with ASTM Standard E2290-07, *Standard Guide for Examination if Handwritten Items*. The opinions expressed in this report were given in accordance with ASTM Standard E1658-07, *Standard Terminology for Expressing Conclusions of Forensic Document Examiners*.

E. Notes:

1. The handwriting samples of Mr. Ross, Ms. Ross, Mr. Williams, and Ms. Davis were taken in my presence and at my direction on February 18, 2008.

2. The original of Document Q1 was examined in the office of the United States Attorney in Macon, Georgia.

3. The documents submitted for examination have been retained in the files of this office pending disposition instructions.

4. My *curriculum vitae* accompanies this report.

Completed this 22ᵑᵈ day of February , 2008.

Farrell C. Shiver
Forensic Document Examiner

Shiver & Nelson
Document Investigation Laboratory, Inc.

1903 Lilac Ridge Drive
Woodstock, GA 30189
770-517-6008
Fax: 678-494-9283

CURRICULUM VITAE

Farrell C. Shiver
Forensic Document Examiner

Education:

Master of Science, Troy State University, Alabama; Criminal Justice, 1983
Bachelor of Science, Jacksonville State University, Alabama; Law Enforcement, 1976

Professional Certification:

American Board of Forensic Document Examiners (ABFDE), certified by testing

Professional Affiliations:

American Society of Questioned Document Examiners (ASQDE), Member
American Academy of Forensic Sciences (AAFS), Questioned Document Section, Member
Southeastern Association of Forensic Document Examiners (SAFDE), Member
Committee E30 on Forensic Sciences and the Questioned Documents Subcommittee,
    ASTM International, Member

Current Positions of Professional Contribution:

- Vice President, American Society of Questioned Document Examiners
- Chairman, Strategic Planning Committee, American Society of Questioned Document
  Examiners
- Participant, Collaborative Testing Services Proficiency Testing Program

Previous Positions of Professional Contribution:

- Chairman, Scientific Working Group for Forensic Document Examination
  Subcommittee on Standard Operating Procedures and Terminology
- Treasurer, Director, and Chairman of Finance Committee, American Society of
  Questioned Document Examiners
- Editor, Journal of the American Society of Questioned Document Examiners
- Member, Executive Committee, Scientific Working Group for Forensic Document
  Examination
- Editor, Southeastern Association of Forensic Document Examiners Newsletter

Curriculum Vitae of Farrell C. Shiver, Forensic Document Examiner
Shiver & Nelson Document Investigation Laboratory, Inc.
Page 2 of 8 Pages

- Chairman, Awards Committee, Southeastern Association of Forensic Document Examiners
- Member, Evaluation and Examination Committee - American Society of Questioned Document Examiners
- Member, Strategic Planning Committee - American Board of Forensic Document Examiners

Professional Experience:

Since 1999, a Forensic Document Examiner in private practice in Woodstock, Georgia, a suburb of Atlanta. Clientele includes attorneys, investigators, corporations, government agencies, and private individuals.

Retired as a Forensic Document Examiner in the United States Army Criminal Investigation Laboratory, Fort Gillem, Georgia. Held positions as Chief of the Questioned Documents Division, as well as Training Officer and Quality Assurance Officer in the Questioned Document Division.

Completed examinations of more than 100,000 items of documentary evidence in over 2000 civil and criminal cases. Provided sworn testimony as an expert witness in the field of Forensic Document Examination on more than 100 occasions in federal, state, and military courts, administrative hearings, and depositions.

Qualification Training:

Graduate of the U.S. Army's Forensic Document Examination Course (1989-1991). This is a two-year resident training program designed to prepare the graduate to serve as an expert witness in the areas of handwriting and hand printing comparison, typewriting, computer printed documents, machine copies, decipherment of altered, obliterated and charred documents, laboratory examinations of inks and paper, decipherment of erased entries and indented writings, detection of counterfeit currency, examination of commercially printed matter and the use of related instrumentation.

Instructional Experience:

Former Training Officer, Questioned Documents Division, U. S. Army Criminal Investigation Laboratory, responsible for administering the two-year course of instruction in forensic document examination. Lectured on numerous occasions on the subject of

Curriculum Vitae of Farrell C. Shiver, Forensic Document Examiner
Shiver & Nelson Document Investigation Laboratory, Inc.
Page 3 of 8 Pages

forensic document examination to groups of investigators of the U.S. Army, U.S. Air Force, U.S. Marine Corps, and a number of civilian law enforcement agencies and to instructors from the Federal Law Enforcement Training Center. Guest lecturer at the U.S. Army Military Police School.

Additional Training Courses, Seminars, and Conferences:

- Annual conferences of the American Society of Questioned Document Examiners (ASQDE), American Academy of Forensic Sciences (AAFS), Southeastern Association of Forensic Document Examiners (SAFDE), and International Association for Identification, Georgia State Division.
- Federal Bureau of Investigation (FBI) - Advanced Techniques of Document Examination for Laboratory Personnel - Typewriters and Other Printing Devices
- FBI - Fundamentals of Document Examination for Laboratory Personnel
- U.S. Secret Service Questioned Document Course
- American Board of Forensic Document Examiners (ABFDE) - Examination Techniques in Handwriting and Rubber Stamp Cases Workshop
- ABFDE - Canon Photocopier, Facsimile, and Microfilm Training Workshop
- Second International Symposium on the Forensic Examination of Questioned Documents
- Rochester Institute of Technology - Orientation to the Graphic Arts
- Mead Corporation - Paper Knowledge Course
- SAFDE - The Examination of Photocopied Signatures; Distinguishing Between Line Quality and Ink Line Morphology Workshop
- SAFDE - The Use of the Haas Atlas CD Compilation Workshop
- SAFDE - Rubber Stamp Plant Tour and Workshop
- SAFDE - Typewriter Identification Workshop
- SAFDE - Signature Workshop
- SAFDE - Difficult Handwriting Workshop
- SAFDE – Fine and Subtle Elements of Handwriting Workshop
- SAFDE - Forensic Examinations of Typographic Documents Workshop
- SAFDE - Examining Documents throughout the Spectrum Workshop
- SAFDE - Production of Genuine Security Documents & the Detection of Counterfeit Documents Workshop
- SAFDE - Disguised Handwriting: An Interactive Workshop
- ASQDE - Fine and Subtle Features of Handwriting Workshop
- ASQDE - Photocopier Identification Workshop

Curriculum Vitae of Farrell C. Shiver, Forensic Document Examiner
Shiver & Nelson Document Investigation Laboratory, Inc.
Page 4 of 8 Pages

- ASQDE - Difficult Handwriting Problems Workshop
- ASQDE - Typewriter Classification and Identification Workshop
- ASQDE - Laser Printer Workshop
- ASQDE - Miscellaneous Document Examination Workshop
- ASQDE & AAFS – Various Signature and Handwriting Workshops
- AAFS - Fraudulent Documents: Their Recognition Workshop
- AAFS - Fraudulent Documents: Their Deterrence Workshop
- AAFS - Digital Forensic Photography
- AAFS - Practical Digital Photography Workshop
- Association of the Pulp and Paper Industry - Papermaking: The Process and the Product
- Canon Corporation - Photocopier Workshop for Law Enforcement
- Canon Corporation - NP-4835 Photocopier Technician's Course
- Canon Corporation - Facsimile Machine Workshop
- Image Enhancement Applications Training
- Imaging and Forensics: New Technologies Workshop
- Bar Code Basics Seminar
- Illinois State Police Laboratory - Fracture Match Workshop
- Tours of U.S. Bureau of Engraving and Printing, paper mills, check printing and
  rubber-stamp producing facilities.

Laboratory Capabilities:

- Microscopy and Photomicrography
- Video Spectral Comparison (Non-destructive testing of inks for infrared reflectance
  and luminescence) with the VSC4
- Electrostatic Document Imaging (Detection of writing impressions and invisible
  writing images) with the ESDA[2]
- Color Computer Imaging and Enhancement

Related Employment:

Nov 1999 through Present – Forensic Document Examiner, Shiver & Nelson Document
Investigation Laboratory, Inc., Woodstock, GA.

Mar 1991 through Nov 1999 – Forensic Document Examiner (and Special Agent), United
States Army Criminal Investigation Laboratory, Fort Gillem, GA

Mar 1989 through Mar 1991 – Student Forensic Document Examiner, (and Special

184

Agent), United States Army Criminal Investigation Laboratory, Fort Gillem, GA.

Mar 1986 through Mar 1989 – Special Agent, U.S. Army CID, Wuerzburg, Germany, with duties as an investigative team chief.

Oct 1983 through Mar 1986 – Special Agent, U.S. Army CID, Fort Ord, CA, with duties as an investigative team chief.

Apr 1981 through Oct 1983 – Special Agent, U.S. Army CID, Fort Benning, GA, with duties as a criminal investigator.

Publications and Presentations:

Scientific Examination of Questioned Documents, 2nd Edition, CRC Press, 2006. Chapter 26, "Accidental Markings and Indented Writings on a Document." Revised chapter previously written by Ordway Hilton.

Nondestructive Differentiation of Full-Color Photocopies, presented at the 1991 conference of the American Academy of Forensic Sciences and published by the Journal of Forensic Sciences, January 1991 (co-author).

Starzecpyzel Rationale Used to Decide U.S. v. Ruth, published by the ABFDE News, October 1995 (co-author).

An Examination of Dry Transfer Lettering as it Related to the Case of an Anonymous Letter, presented at the 1989 conference of the Southeastern Association of Forensic Document Examiners.

Chemical Enhancement of Faint NCR Paper Writing Images, presented at the 1990 conference of the American Society of Questioned Document Examiners and the 1990 conference of the Southeastern Association of Forensic Document Examiners.

Off-set Marks and Printing Ink Smears, How Reliable in the Identification of a Photocopy to an Original Document? presented at the 1991 conference of the Southeastern Association of Forensic Document Examiners.

NCR Paper, Damage Detection Agent and the Latent Print Examiner, presented at the 1991 conference of the Georgia State Division of the International Association for

Curriculum Vitae of Farrell C. Shiver, Forensic Document Examiner
Shiver & Nelson Document Investigation Laboratory, Inc.
Page 6 of 8 Pages

Identification.

Dry Transfer Lettering and the Anonymous Note, presented at the 1991 conference of the American Society of Questioned Document Examiners (co-author).

Questioned Document Training in the U.S. Army Criminal Investigation Laboratory, presented at the 1992 conference of the American Academy of Forensic Sciences.

Was the Second Page Inserted? presented at the 1992 conference of the Southeastern Association of Forensic Document Examiners.

Additional Applications for Damage Detection Agent for CB Coatings, presented at the 1992 conference of the American Society of Questioned Document Examiners.

RAW O? How to Construct an Inexpensive Device to Assist in the Reading of Typewriter Ribbons, presented at the 1993 conference of the Southeastern Association of Forensic Document Examiners.

Subject A or Subject B? presented at the 1994 conference of the Southeastern Association of Forensic Document Examiners.

Photocopier Identification: Discussion of a Problem Associated with Multi-Generation Photocopies, presented at the 1994 conference of the American Society of Questioned Document Examiners.

A Guide for Civilian Document Examiners Testifying in Courts-Martial, presented at the 1995 conference of the American Academy of Forensic Sciences.

The New Military Identification Card, presented at the 1995 conference of the Southeastern Association of Forensic Document Examiners.

Case Report: The Value of Field Assistance to the Investigator in a Counterfeit Check Case, presented at the 1996 conference of the Southeastern Association of Forensic Document Examiners.

Case Report: The Individuality of Handwriting Demonstrated through the Field Screening of 1000 Writers, presented at the 1996 conference of the American Society of Questioned Document Examiners.

Curriculum Vitae of Farrell C. Shiver, Forensic Document Examiner
Shiver & Nelson Document Investigation Laboratory, Inc.
Page 7 of 8 Pages

The "Expert" Critic, presented at the 1997 conference of the American Society of Questioned Document Examiners.

Examination of the Postal Identification Tag, presented at the 1998 conference of the Southeastern Association of Forensic Document Examiners.

A Comparison of the FontFinder and FontExpert Typeface Recognition Programs, presented at the 1999 conference of the Southeastern Association of Forensic Document Examiners.

Risograph Revisited, presented at the 2000 conference of the Southeastern Association of Forensic Document Examiners.

What's the Difference? presented at the 2001 conferences of the American Society of Questioned Document Examiners and the Southeastern Association of Forensic Document Examiners.

Forensic Document Examination in Medical Malpractice Cases, presented at the Medical Malpractice Institute, Sea Island, GA, November 16, 2001.

Secondary Impressions from Mailing Envelopes, presented at the 2002 conference of the American Academy of Forensic Sciences.

Daubert in the SAFDE States, presented at the 2003 conference of the Southeastern Association of Forensic Document Examiners.

Daubert in the State Courts, presented at the 2003 conference of the American Society of Questioned Document Examiners.

The Electrostatic Decipherment of a Liquid-Damaged Ink Entry, presented at the 2004 conference of the Southeastern Association of Forensic Document Examiners.

Daubert in the SAFDE States- 1st Update, presented at the 2004 conference of the Southeastern Association of Forensic Document Examiners.

A Comparison of the ESDA^2 to the ESDA: Including an Evaluation of the Toner Application Device (TAD) Method vs. Cascade Development Method, presented at the 2005 conference of the Southeastern Association of Forensic Document Examiners.

Curriculum Vitae of Farrell C. Shiver, Forensic Document Examiner
Shiver & Nelson Document Investigation Laboratory, Inc.
Page 8 of 8 Pages

The Forensic Examination of Documents Produced by Computer Printers, Facsimile Machines, and Photocopiers, presented at the 2006 CyberCrime Summit at Kennesaw State University, GA.

Daubert in the SAFDE States- 2nd Update, presented at the 2006 conference of the Southeastern Association of Forensic Document Examiners.

Paper Basis Weight and the Creation of Secondary Impressions, presented at the 2007 conference of the Southeastern Association of Forensic Document Examiners.

A Current Look at the Pitfalls in the Use of Ultraviolet Examination to Differentiate between Writing Papers, presented at the 2007 conference of the Southeastern Association of Forensic Document Examiners.

For Products, Public Speaking Request, Guest
Appearances, Media Interviews, endorsements, and
consultation services, please contact:
Name:
Address: 3588 HWY 138 SE,#442, Stockbridge Ga,
30281
Phone Number:
Fax Number:
Email Address: Princersc@yahoo.com
Website:
Social Media: